Keeping Up With The Jacksons:

A Financial Management Guide for American Teens

Suzanne Kleinberg

Other Books by Suzanne Kleinberg

From Playstation® to Workstation: A Career Guide for Generation Text Surviving in a Baby Boomer World.

Employee Rights and Employer Wrongs: How To Identify Employee Abuse and How To Stand Up For Yourself.

Keeping Up With The Jacksons:

A Financial Management Guide for American Teens

Suzanne Kleinberg

Potential To Soar Publishing
Toronto, Canada

Cover images used and altered with the permission of the Federal Reserve.

Canadian Cataloguing in Publication Data

Library and Archives Canada Cataloguing in Publication

Kleinberg, Suzanne, 1963-
    Keeping Up With The Jacksons : A Financial Management Guide For American Teens / Suzanne Kleinberg .

Includes index.
ISBN 978-0-9916861-0-0

    1. Teenagers--Finance, Personal. 2. Finance, Personal.

Potential To Soar Publishing
Thornhill, Ontario

Dedication

To my mother, Frances, a woman before her time, who instilled in me early on that success and independence cannot come without financial responsibility.

Table of Contents

Introduction

"If you think nobody cares if you are alive,
try missing a couple of car payments."
-- Anonymous

Remember when your only financial concern was making your allowance last the whole week? Well, those days are over! As you approach adulthood, you are responsible for managing your own finances. The sooner you gain control, the more skilled you will be at avoiding common pitfalls that could have you enslaved in debt for years. If you get manage your finances and understand them now, then you will have a lot less stress later on.

Some people hate planning but it is vital that you prepare yourself financially. As we age, expenses tend to increase...from kids who want toys; to teens who want iPhones; to adults buying a home ....and so on. Unexpected things happen all the time - so being financially prepared makes life much less stressful. If you plan now, you won't have to grovel to friends and family later.

Sounds easy? Well, clearly it is not when you look at some of the statistics on debt for young adults. (Sources: Charles Schwab US 2011 and Sallie Mae 2009)

- On average, 30% of the monthly income of young adults between 18-24 years old goes to debt repayment (i.e. credit card interest, car or student loan interest, etc.).
- 29% of teens are in debt.
- College students carry an average of $27,000 in debt ($24,000 in student loans, $3000 in credit card debt).
- 39% of teens know how to manage a credit card (as opposed to 64% in 2007) yet only 32% understand credit card interest charges and fees (as opposed to 43% in 2007).
- 7-10% of undergraduates drop out due to debt problems.
- Only 33% of teens know how to read a bank statement, balance a check book and pay bills.
- 91% of undergraduates have at least one credit card, up from 76% in 2004. The average number of cards has grown to 4.6, with half of college students having four or more cards.
- Only 20% of teens know how to invest money.
- The number of people between 18-24 years old who have declared bankruptcy in 2007 has increased 96% in ten years.
- Teens' salary expectations are at $70,000 for their starting salary and $150,000 for their salary once they are established in their career. With these expectations being so far out of line from reality, it may be a contributing factor to their high spending and high debt.

In this book, we will review a lot of the realities about income and expenses as well as savings and investments. At the end, you will have the opportunity to put together a budget to understand your current financial snapshot.

Preface

Money, money, money! It appears that a lot of us in today's society can never get enough. However, in most cases, the problem is not that we don't have enough; it is that we don't know how to effectively manage it. As a result, Americans are experiencing record levels of debt. High levels of debt impact us all.

This is why it is essential that young Americans learn the importance of financial planning long before they are out on their own. Without this knowledge, mistakes could lead them into serious money troubles including credit problems, collection agency harassment, identity theft and/or bankruptcy.

To avoid today's problems, teens need to know more than just putting money into a savings account for a rainy day. They need to understand all the options and the pitfalls out there. They need to understand not only the importance of a budget but how to effectively complete one. They need to have a clear vision of what it costs to live on your own in an American city. They also definitely need to know about taxes and how much of their income it can eat away.

Currently, there are few publications available specifically for teens in the marketplace. Through practical examples and exercises, teens can easily gain confidence in the key basics of money management. This book was written to address the gap in the accessibility of this information and to provide useful exercises so that the upcoming generation does not repeat the missteps of the current generation.

What You Earn Is Not What You Get

Salary and Taxes

It is always exciting to get a new job that pays more than the last one. However, the joy seems to fade when we get our first paycheck and see all the taxes and the costs of company benefits taken off. *Before* you get any paycheck, whether it is an actual check or deposited in your bank account by your employer (known as "direct deposit"), it is required by law that your employer withdraw taxes owed prior to paying you. So don't be shocked if you start your first job expecting a big check after your first two weeks on the job and see something totally different in your bank account.

In the American tax code, the more you earn, the higher your tax rate. In the table below, you will see that the higher salary pays a higher tax rate. States independently set their own tax rates. Some have implemented varying rates based on salary, while others have a flat rate or no state tax at all.

There is no difference in tax rates if you are a salaried employee (i.e. full time with a determined yearly salary) vs. a part time employee who gets an hourly wage. The tax rate is based on the expected total income for the full calendar year. Here are **2012** examples for each state:

Alabama

	Example A	Example B	Example C
Annual Income	$26,000.00	$52,000.00	$100,000.00
Gross **weekly** pay	**$500.00**	**$1,000.00**	**$1,923.08**
Federal Tax	$75.00	$250.00	$538.46
State Tax	$25.00	$50.00	$96.15
Soc. Sec. (4.2% up to $6,826.20)	$21.00	$42.00	$80.77
Medicare (1.45%)	$7.25	$14.50	$27.88
*Net Amount**	**$371.75**	**$643.50**	**$1,179.82**

Alaska

	Example A	Example B	Example C
Annual Income	$26,000.00	$52,000.00	$100,000.00
Gross **weekly** pay	**$500.00**	**$1,000.00**	**$1,923.08**
Federal Tax	$75.00	$250.00	$538.46
State Tax	$0.00	$0.00	$0.00
Soc. Sec. (4.2% up to $6,826.20)	$21.00	$42.00	$80.77
Medicare (1.45%)	$7.25	$14.50	$27.88
*Net Amount**	**$396.75**	**$693.50**	**$1,275.97**

Arkansas

	Example A	Example B	Example C
Annual Income	$26,000.00	$52,000.00	$100,000.00
Gross **weekly** pay	**$500.00**	**$1,000.00**	**$1,923.08**
Federal Tax	$75.00	$250.00	$538.46
State Tax	$30.00	$70.00	$134.62
Soc. Sec. (4.2% up to $6,826.20)	$21.00	$42.00	$80.77
Medicare (1.45%)	$7.25	$14.50	$27.88
*Net Amount**	**$366.75**	**$623.50**	**$1,141.35**

Arizona

	Example A	Example B	Example C
Annual Income	$26,000.00	$52,000.00	$100,000.00
Gross **weekly** pay	**$500.00**	**$1,000.00**	**$1,923.08**
Federal Tax	$75.00	$250.00	$538.46
State Tax	$0.00	$0.00	$0.00
Soc. Sec. (4.2% up to $6,826.20)	$21.00	$42.00	$80.77
Medicare (1.45%)	$7.25	$14.50	$27.88
*Net Amount**	**$396.75**	**$693.50**	**$1,275.97**

California

	Example A	Example B	Example C
Annual Income	$26,000.00	$52,000.00	$100,000.00
Gross **weekly** pay	**$500.00**	**$1,000.00**	**$1,923.08**
Federal Tax	$75.00	$250.00	$538.46
State Tax	$30.00	$93.00	$178.85
Soc. Sec. (4.2% up to $6,826.20)	$21.00	$42.00	$80.77
Medicare (1.45%)	$7.25	$14.50	$27.88
*Net Amount**	**$366.75**	**$600.50**	**$1,097.12**

Colorado

	Example A	Example B	Example C
Annual Income	$26,000.00	$52,000.00	$100,000.00
Gross **weekly** pay	**$500.00**	**$1,000.00**	**$1,923.08**
Federal Tax	$75.00	$250.00	$538.46
State Tax	$23.15	$46.30	$89.04
Soc. Sec. (4.2% up to $6,826.20)	$21.00	$42.00	$80.77
Medicare (1.45%)	$7.25	$14.50	$27.88
*Net Amount**	**$373.60**	**$647.20**	**$1,186.93**

Connecticut

	Example A	Example B	Example C
Annual Income	$26,000.00	$52,000.00	$100,000.00
Gross **weekly** pay	**$500.00**	**$1,000.00**	**$1,923.08**
Federal Tax	$75.00	$250.00	$538.46
State Tax	$25.00	$55.00	$115.39
Soc. Sec. (4.2% up to $6,826.20)	$21.00	$42.00	$80.77
Medicare (1.45%)	$7.25	$14.50	$27.88
*Net Amount**	**$371.75**	**$638.50**	**$1,160.58**

Delaware

	Example A	Example B	Example C
Annual Income	$26,000.00	$52,000.00	$100,000.00
Gross **weekly** pay	**$500.00**	**$1,000.00**	**$1,923.08**
Federal Tax	$75.00	$250.00	$538.46
State Tax	$27.50	$55.00	$133.65
Soc. Sec. (4.2% up to $6,826.20)	$21.00	$42.00	$80.77
Medicare (1.45%)	$7.25	$14.50	$27.88
*Net Amount**	**$369.25**	**$638.50**	**$1,142.32**

District of Columbia

	Example A	Example B	Example C
Annual Income	$26,000.00	$52,000.00	$100,000.00
Gross **weekly** pay	**$500.00**	**$1,000.00**	**$1,923.08**
Federal Tax	$75.00	$250.00	$538.46
State Tax	$30.00	$85.00	$163.46
Soc. Sec. (4.2% up to $6,826.20)	$21.00	$42.00	$80.77
Medicare (1.45%)	$7.25	$14.50	$27.88
*Net Amount**	**$366.75**	**$608.50**	**$1,112.51**

Florida

	Example A	Example B	Example C
Annual Income	$26,000.00	$52,000.00	$100,000.00
Gross **weekly** pay	**$500.00**	**$1,000.00**	**$1,923.08**
Federal Tax	$75.00	$250.00	$538.46
State Tax	$0.00	$0.00	$0.00
Soc. Sec. (4.2% up to $6,826.20)	$21.00	$42.00	$80.77
Medicare (1.45%)	$7.25	$14.50	$27.88
*Net Amount**	**$396.75**	**$693.50**	**$1,275.97**

Georgia

	Example A	Example B	Example C
Annual Income	$26,000.00	$52,000.00	$100,000.00
Gross **weekly** pay	**$500.00**	**$1,000.00**	**$1,923.08**
Federal Tax	$75.00	$250.00	$538.46
State Tax	$30.00	$60.00	$115.38
Soc. Sec. (4.2% up to $6,826.20)	$21.00	$42.00	$80.77
Medicare (1.45%)	$7.25	$14.50	$27.88
*Net Amount**	**$366.75**	**$633.50**	**$1,160.59**

Hawaii

	Example A	Example B	Example C
Annual Income	$26,000.00	$52,000.00	$100,000.00
Gross **weekly** pay	**$500.00**	**$1,000.00**	**$1,923.08**
Federal Tax	$75.00	$250.00	$538.46
State Tax	$38.00	$82.50	$158.65
Soc. Sec. (4.2% up to $6,826.20)	$21.00	$42.00	$80.77
Medicare (1.45%)	$7.25	$14.50	$27.88
*Net Amount**	**$358.75**	**$611.00**	**$1,117.32**

Idaho

	Example A	Example B	Example C
Annual Income	$26,000.00	$52,000.00	$100,000.00
Gross **weekly** pay	**$500.00**	**$1,000.00**	**$1,923.08**
Federal Tax	$75.00	$250.00	$538.46
State Tax	$39.00	$78.00	$150.00
Soc. Sec. (4.2% up to $6,826.20)	$21.00	$42.00	$80.77
Medicare (1.45%)	$7.25	$14.50	$27.88
*Net Amount**	**$357.75**	**$615.50**	**$1,125.97**

Illinois

	Example A	Example B	Example C
Annual Income	$26,000.00	$52,000.00	$100,000.00
Gross **weekly** pay	**$500.00**	**$1,000.00**	**$1,923.08**
Federal Tax	$75.00	$250.00	$538.46
State Tax	$25.00	$50.00	$96.15
Soc. Sec. (4.2% up to $6,826.20)	$21.00	$42.00	$80.77
Medicare (1.45%)	$7.25	$14.50	$27.88
*Net Amount**	**$371.75**	**$643.50**	**$1,179.82**

Indiana

	Example A	Example B	Example C
Annual Income	$26,000.00	$52,000.00	$100,000.00
Gross **weekly** pay	**$500.00**	**$1,000.00**	**$1,923.08**
Federal Tax	$75.00	$250.00	$538.46
State Tax	$17.00	$34.00	$65.38
Soc. Sec. (4.2% up to $6,826.20)	$21.00	$42.00	$80.77
Medicare (1.45%)	$7.25	$14.50	$27.88
*Net Amount**	**$379.75**	**$659.50**	**$1,210.59**

Iowa

	Example A	Example B	Example C
Annual Income	$26,000.00	$52,000.00	$100,000.00
Gross **weekly** pay	**$500.00**	**$1,000.00**	**$1,923.08**
Federal Tax	$75.00	$250.00	$538.46
State Tax	$32.40	$79.20	$172.69
Soc. Sec. (4.2% up to $6,826.20)	$21.00	$42.00	$80.77
Medicare (1.45%)	$7.25	$14.50	$27.88
*Net Amount**	**$364.35**	**$614.30**	**$1,103.28**

Kansas

	Example A	Example B	Example C
Annual Income	$26,000.00	$52,000.00	$100,000.00
Gross **weekly** pay	**$500.00**	**$1,000.00**	**$1,923.08**
Federal Tax	$75.00	$250.00	$538.46
State Tax	$31.25	$64.50	$124.04
Soc. Sec. (4.2% up to $6,826.20)	$21.00	$42.00	$80.77
Medicare (1.45%)	$7.25	$14.50	$27.88
*Net Amount**	**$365.50**	**$629.00**	**$1,151.93**

Kentucky

	Example A	Example B	Example C
Annual Income	$26,000.00	$52,000.00	$100,000.00
Gross **weekly** pay	**$500.00**	**$1,000.00**	**$1,923.08**
Federal Tax	$75.00	$250.00	$538.46
State Tax	$29.00	$58.00	$115.39
Soc. Sec. (4.2% up to $6,826.20)	$21.00	$42.00	$80.77
Medicare (1.45%)	$7.25	$14.50	$27.88
*Net Amount**	**$367.75**	**$635.50**	**$1,160.58**

Louisiana

	Example A	Example B	Example C
Annual Income	$26,000.00	$52,000.00	$100,000.00
Gross **weekly** pay	**$500.00**	**$1,000.00**	**$1,923.08**
Federal Tax	$75.00	$250.00	$538.46
State Tax	$20.00	$60.00	$153.85
Soc. Sec. (4.2% up to $6,826.20)	$21.00	$42.00	$80.77
Medicare (1.45%)	$7.25	$14.50	$27.88
*Net Amount**	**$376.75**	**$633.50**	**$1,122.12**

Maine

	Example A	Example B	Example C
Annual Income	$26,000.00	$52,000.00	$100,000.00
Gross **weekly** pay	**$500.00**	**$1,000.00**	**$1,923.08**
Federal Tax	$75.00	$250.00	$538.46
State Tax	$42.50	$85.00	$163.46
Soc. Sec. (4.2% up to $6,826.20)	$21.00	$42.00	$80.77
Medicare (1.45%)	$7.25	$14.50	$27.88
*Net Amount**	**$354.25**	**$608.50**	**$1,112.51**

Maryland

	Example A	Example B	Example C
Annual Income	$26,000.00	$52,000.00	$100,000.00
Gross **weekly** pay	**$500.00**	**$1,000.00**	**$1,923.08**
Federal Tax	$75.00	$250.00	$538.46
State Tax	$23.75	$47.50	$96.15
Soc. Sec. (4.2% up to $6,826.20)	$21.00	$42.00	$80.77
Medicare (1.45%)	$7.25	$14.50	$27.88
*Net Amount**	**$373.00**	**$646.00**	**$1,179.82**

Massachusetts

	Example A	Example B	Example C
Annual Income	$26,000.00	$52,000.00	$100,000.00
Gross **weekly** pay	**$500.00**	**$1,000.00**	**$1,923.08**
Federal Tax	$75.00	$250.00	$538.46
State Tax	$26.50	$53.00	$101.92
Soc. Sec. (4.2% up to $6,826.20)	$21.00	$42.00	$80.77
Medicare (1.45%)	$7.25	$14.50	$27.88
Net Amount*	**$370.25**	**$640.50**	**$1,174.05**

Michigan

	Example A	Example B	Example C
Annual Income	$26,000.00	$52,000.00	$100,000.00
Gross **weekly** pay	**$500.00**	**$1,000.00**	**$1,923.08**
Federal Tax	$75.00	$250.00	$538.46
State Tax	$21.75	$43.50	$83.65
Soc. Sec. (4.2% up to $6,826.20)	$21.00	$42.00	$80.77
Medicare (1.45%)	$7.25	$14.50	$27.88
Net Amount*	**$375.00**	**$650.00**	**$1,192.32**

Minnesota

	Example A	Example B	Example C
Annual Income	$26,000.00	$52,000.00	$100,000.00
Gross **weekly** pay	**$500.00**	**$1,000.00**	**$1,923.08**
Federal Tax	$75.00	$250.00	$538.46
State Tax	$35.00	$70.00	$150.96
Soc. Sec. (4.2% up to $6,826.20)	$21.00	$42.00	$80.77
Medicare (1.45%)	$7.25	$14.50	$27.88
Net Amount*	**$361.75**	**$623.50**	**$1,125.01**

Mississippi

	Example A	Example B	Example C
Annual Income	$26,000.00	$52,000.00	$100,000.00
Gross **weekly** pay	**$500.00**	**$1,000.00**	**$1,923.08**
Federal Tax	$75.00	$250.00	$538.46
State Tax	$25.00	$50.00	$96.15
Soc. Sec. (4.2% up to $6,826.20)	$21.00	$42.00	$80.77
Medicare (1.45%)	$7.25	$14.50	$27.88
Net Amount*	**$371.75**	**$643.50**	**$1,179.82**

Missouri

	Example A	Example B	Example C
Annual Income	$26,000.00	$52,000.00	$100,000.00
Gross **weekly** pay	**$500.00**	**$1,000.00**	**$1,923.08**
Federal Tax	$75.00	$250.00	$538.46
State Tax	$30.00	$60.00	$115.39
Soc. Sec. (4.2% up to $6,826.20)	$21.00	$42.00	$80.77
Medicare (1.45%)	$7.25	$14.50	$27.88
*Net Amount**	**$366.75**	**$633.50**	**$1,160.58**

Montana

	Example A	Example B	Example C
Annual Income	$26,000.00	$52,000.00	$100,000.00
Gross **weekly** pay	**$500.00**	**$1,000.00**	**$1,923.08**
Federal Tax	$75.00	$250.00	$538.46
State Tax	$34.50	$69.00	$132.69
Soc. Sec. (4.2% up to $6,826.20)	$21.00	$42.00	$80.77
Medicare (1.45%)	$7.25	$14.50	$27.88
*Net Amount**	**$362.25**	**$624.50**	**$1,143.28**

Nebraska

	Example A	Example B	Example C
Annual Income	$26,000.00	$52,000.00	$100,000.00
Gross **weekly** pay	**$500.00**	**$1,000.00**	**$1,923.08**
Federal Tax	$75.00	$250.00	$538.46
State Tax	$25.60	$68.40	$131.54
Soc. Sec. (4.2% up to $6,826.20)	$21.00	$42.00	$80.77
Medicare (1.45%)	$7.25	$14.50	$27.88
*Net Amount**	**$371.15**	**$625.10**	**$1,144.43**

Nevada

	Example A	Example B	Example C
Annual Income	$26,000.00	$52,000.00	$100,000.00
Gross **weekly** pay	**$500.00**	**$1,000.00**	**$1,923.08**
Federal Tax	$75.00	$250.00	$538.46
State Tax	$0.00	$0.00	$0.00
Soc. Sec. (4.2% up to $6,826.20)	$21.00	$42.00	$80.77
Medicare (1.45%)	$7.25	$14.50	$27.88
*Net Amount**	**$396.75**	**$693.50**	**$1,275.97**

New Hampshire

	Example A	Example B	Example C
Annual Income	$26,000.00	$52,000.00	$100,000.00
Gross **weekly** pay	**$500.00**	**$1,000.00**	**$1,923.08**
Federal Tax	$75.00	$250.00	$538.46
State Tax	$0.00	$0.00	$0.00
Soc. Sec. (4.2% up to $6,826.20)	$21.00	$42.00	$80.77
Medicare (1.45%)	$7.25	$14.50	$27.88
*Net Amount**	**$396.75**	**$693.50**	**$1,275.97**

New Jersey

	Example A	Example B	Example C
Annual Income	$26,000.00	$52,000.00	$100,000.00
Gross **weekly** pay	**$500.00**	**$1,000.00**	**$1,923.08**
Federal Tax	$75.00	$250.00	$538.46
State Tax	$8.75	$55.25	$121.15
Soc. Sec. (4.2% up to $6,826.20)	$21.00	$42.00	$80.77
Medicare (1.45%)	$7.25	$14.50	$27.88
*Net Amount**	**$388.00**	**$638.25**	**$1,154.82**

New Mexico

	Example A	Example B	Example C
Annual Income	$26,000.00	$52,000.00	$100,000.00
Gross **weekly** pay	**$500.00**	**$1,000.00**	**$1,923.08**
Federal Tax	$75.00	$250.00	$538.46
State Tax	$24.50	$49.00	$94.23
Soc. Sec. (4.2% up to $6,826.20)	$21.00	$42.00	$80.77
Medicare (1.45%)	$7.25	$14.50	$27.88
*Net Amount**	**$372.25**	**$644.50**	**$1,181.74**

New York

	Example A	Example B	Example C
Annual Income	$26,000.00	$52,000.00	$100,000.00
Gross **weekly** pay	**$500.00**	**$1,000.00**	**$1,923.08**
Federal Tax	$75.00	$250.00	$538.46
State Tax	$32.25	$64.50	$127.88
Soc. Sec. (4.2% up to $6,826.20)	$21.00	$42.00	$80.77
Medicare (1.45%)	$7.25	$14.50	$27.88
*Net Amount**	**$364.50**	**$629.00**	**$1,148.09**

North Carolina

	Example A	Example B	Example C
Annual Income	$26,000.00	$52,000.00	$100,000.00
Gross **weekly** pay	**$500.00**	**$1,000.00**	**$1,923.08**
Federal Tax	$75.00	$250.00	$538.46
State Tax	$35.00	$70.00	$149.04
Soc. Sec. (4.2% up to $6,826.20)	$21.00	$42.00	$80.77
Medicare (1.45%)	$7.25	$14.50	$27.88
*Net Amount**	**$361.75**	**$623.50**	**$1,126.93**

North Dakota

	Example A	Example B	Example C
Annual Income	$26,000.00	$52,000.00	$100,000.00
Gross **weekly** pay	**$500.00**	**$1,000.00**	**$1,923.08**
Federal Tax	$75.00	$250.00	$538.46
State Tax	$7.55	$28.20	$60.19
Soc. Sec. (4.2% up to $6,826.20)	$21.00	$42.00	$80.77
Medicare (1.45%)	$7.25	$14.50	$27.88
*Net Amount**	**$389.20**	**$665.30**	**$1,215.78**

Ohio

	Example A	Example B	Example C
Annual Income	$26,000.00	$52,000.00	$100,000.00
Gross **weekly** pay	**$500.00**	**$1,000.00**	**$1,923.08**
Federal Tax	$75.00	$250.00	$538.46
State Tax	$17.61	$41.09	$90.29
Soc. Sec. (4.2% up to $6,826.20)	$21.00	$42.00	$80.77
Medicare (1.45%)	$7.25	$14.50	$27.88
*Net Amount**	**$379.14**	**$652.41**	**$1,185.68**

Oklahoma

	Example A	Example B	Example C
Annual Income	$26,000.00	$52,000.00	$100,000.00
Gross **weekly** pay	**$500.00**	**$1,000.00**	**$1,923.08**
Federal Tax	$75.00	$250.00	$538.46
State Tax	$27.50	$55.00	$105.77
Soc. Sec. (4.2% up to $6,826.20)	$21.00	$42.00	$80.77
Medicare (1.45%)	$7.25	$14.50	$27.88
*Net Amount**	**$369.25**	**$638.50**	**$1,170.20**

Oregon

	Example A	Example B	Example C
Annual Income	$26,000.00	$52,000.00	$100,000.00
Gross **weekly** pay	**$500.00**	**$1,000.00**	**$1,923.08**
Federal Tax	$75.00	$250.00	$538.46
State Tax	$45.00	$90.00	$173.08
Soc. Sec. (4.2% up to $6,826.20)	$21.00	$42.00	$80.77
Medicare (1.45%)	$7.25	$14.50	$27.88
*Net Amount**	**$351.75**	**$603.50**	**$1,102.89**

Pennsylvania

	Example A	Example B	Example C
Annual Income	$26,000.00	$52,000.00	$100,000.00
Gross **weekly** pay	**$500.00**	**$1,000.00**	**$1,923.08**
Federal Tax	$75.00	$250.00	$538.46
State Tax	$15.35	$30.70	$59.04
Soc. Sec. (4.2% up to $6,826.20)	$21.00	$42.00	$80.77
Medicare (1.45%)	$7.25	$14.50	$27.88
*Net Amount**	**$381.40**	**$662.80**	**$1,216.93**

Rhode Island

	Example A	Example B	Example C
Annual Income	$26,000.00	$52,000.00	$100,000.00
Gross **weekly** pay	**$500.00**	**$1,000.00**	**$1,923.08**
Federal Tax	$75.00	$250.00	$538.46
State Tax	$18.75	$37.50	$91.35
Soc. Sec. (4.2% up to $6,826.20)	$21.00	$42.00	$80.77
Medicare (1.45%)	$7.25	$14.50	$27.88
*Net Amount**	**$378.00**	**$656.00**	**$1,184.62**

South Carolina

	Example A	Example B	Example C
Annual Income	$26,000.00	$52,000.00	$100,000.00
Gross **weekly** pay	**$500.00**	**$1,000.00**	**$1,923.08**
Federal Tax	$75.00	$250.00	$538.46
State Tax	$35.00	$70.00	$134.62
Soc. Sec. (4.2% up to $6,826.20)	$21.00	$42.00	$80.77
Medicare (1.45%)	$7.25	$14.50	$27.88
*Net Amount**	**$361.75**	**$623.50**	**$1,788.46**

South Dakota

	Example A	Example B	Example C
Annual Income	$26,000.00	$52,000.00	$100,000.00
Gross **weekly** pay	**$500.00**	**$1,000.00**	**$1,923.08**
Federal Tax	$75.00	$250.00	$538.46
State Tax	$0.00	$0.00	$0.00
Soc. Sec. (4.2% up to $6,826.20)	$21.00	$42.00	$80.77
Medicare (1.45%)	$7.25	$14.50	$27.88
*Net Amount**	**$396.75**	**$693.50**	**$1,275.97**

Tennessee

	Example A	Example B	Example C
Annual Income	$26,000.00	$52,000.00	$100,000.00
Gross **weekly** pay	**$500.00**	**$1,000.00**	**$1,923.08**
Federal Tax	$75.00	$250.00	$538.46
State Tax	$0.00	$0.00	$0.00
Soc. Sec. (4.2% up to $6,826.20)	$21.00	$42.00	$80.77
Medicare (1.45%)	$7.25	$14.50	$27.88
*Net Amount**	**$396.75**	**$693.50**	**$1,275.97**

Texas

	Example A	Example B	Example C
Annual Income	$26,000.00	$52,000.00	$100,000.00
Gross **weekly** pay	**$500.00**	**$1,000.00**	**$1,923.08**
Federal Tax	$75.00	$250.00	$538.46
State Tax	$0.00	$0.00	$0.00
Soc. Sec. (4.2% up to $6,826.20)	$21.00	$42.00	$80.77
Medicare (1.45%)	$7.25	$14.50	$27.88
*Net Amount**	**$396.75**	**$693.50**	**$1,275.97**

Utah

	Example A	Example B	Example C
Annual Income	$26,000.00	$52,000.00	$100,000.00
Gross **weekly** pay	**$500.00**	**$1,000.00**	**$1,923.08**
Federal Tax	$75.00	$250.00	$538.46
State Tax	$25.00	$50.00	$96.15
Soc. Sec. (4.2% up to $6,826.20)	$21.00	$42.00	$80.77
Medicare (1.45%)	$7.25	$14.50	$27.88
*Net Amount**	**$371.75**	**$643.50**	**$1,179.82**

Vermont

	Example A	Example B	Example C
Annual Income	$26,000.00	$52,000.00	$100,000.00
Gross **weekly** pay	**$500.00**	**$1,000.00**	**$1,923.08**
Federal Tax	$75.00	$250.00	$538.46
State Tax	$17.75	$68.00	$150.00
Soc. Sec. (4.2% up to $6,826.20)	$21.00	$42.00	$80.77
Medicare (1.45%)	$7.25	$14.50	$27.88
*Net Amount**	**$379.00**	**$625.50**	**$1,125.97**

Virginia

	Example A	Example B	Example C
Annual Income	$26,000.00	$52,000.00	$100,000.00
Gross **weekly** pay	**$500.00**	**$1,000.00**	**$1,923.08**
Federal Tax	$75.00	$250.00	$538.46
State Tax	$28.75	$57.50	$110.58
Soc. Sec. (4.2% up to $6,826.20)	$21.00	$42.00	$80.77
Medicare (1.45%)	$7.25	$14.50	$27.88
*Net Amount**	**$368.00**	**$636.00**	**$1,165.39**

West Virginia

	Example A	Example B	Example C
Annual Income	$26,000.00	$52,000.00	$100,000.00
Gross **weekly** pay	**$500.00**	**$1,000.00**	**$1,923.08**
Federal Tax	$75.00	$250.00	$538.46
State Tax	$22.50	$60.00	$125.00
Soc. Sec. (4.2% up to $6,826.20)	$21.00	$42.00	$80.77
Medicare (1.45%)	$7.25	$14.50	$27.88
*Net Amount**	**$374.25**	**$633.50**	**$1,150.97**

Washington

	Example A	Example B	Example C
Annual Income	$26,000.00	$52,000.00	$100,000.00
Gross **weekly** pay	**$500.00**	**$1,000.00**	**$1,923.08**
Federal Tax	$75.00	$250.00	$538.46
State Tax	$0.00	$0.00	$0.00
Soc. Sec. (4.2% up to $6,826.20)	$21.00	$42.00	$80.77
Medicare (1.45%)	$7.25	$14.50	$27.88
*Net Amount**	**$396.75**	**$693.50**	**$1,275.97**

Wisconsin

	Example A	Example B	Example C
Annual Income	$26,000.00	$52,000.00	$100,000.00
Gross **weekly** pay	**$500.00**	**$1,000.00**	**$1,923.08**
Federal Tax	$75.00	$250.00	$538.46
State Tax	$32.50	$65.00	$125.00
Soc. Sec. (4.2% up to $6,826.20)	$21.00	$42.00	$80.77
Medicare (1.45%)	$7.25	$14.50	$27.88
*Net Amount**	**$364.25**	**$628.50**	**$1,150.97**

Wyoming

	Example A	Example B	Example C
Annual Income	$26,000.00	$52,000.00	$100,000.00
Gross **weekly** pay	**$500.00**	**$1,000.00**	**$1,923.08**
Federal Tax	$75.00	$250.00	$538.46
State Tax	$0.00	$0.00	$0.00
Soc. Sec. (4.2% up to $6,826.20)	$21.00	$42.00	$80.77
Medicare (1.45%)	$7.25	$14.50	$27.88
*Net Amount**	**$396.75**	**$693.50**	**$1,275.97**

*Does *not* include costs of company pensions, benefits, or insurance that is withdrawn from your pay.

Social Security (U.S. Pension Plan) is money from the government that you will receive monthly after age 65 similar to a salary as well as workers who become disabled and families in which a spouse or parent dies. The amount you receive depends on the amount that you have paid into the system throughout the years. The money you pay in taxes is not held in a personal account for you to use when you get benefits. Your taxes are being used right now to pay people who now are getting benefits. Any unused money goes to the Social Security trust funds, not a personal account with your name on it. For more information: http://www.ssa.gov/

Medicare is basic health insurance program for people age 65 or older and many people with disabilities. You should not confuse Medicare and Medicaid. Medicaid is a health care program for people with low income and limited resources usually run by state welfare or social services agencies. For more information: http://www.socialsecurity.gov/pubs/10043.html

These deductions may be displayed as "FICA" on your pay stub. FICA stands for Federal Insurance Contributions Act which is the law that requires a deduction from paychecks and income that goes toward the Social Security program and Medicare.

Don't assume that these taxes are the total amount of tax that you will be accountable for. If your employer underestimates your annual earnings (e.g. if you get a bonus or a raise during the year), then you may be required to pay more taxes when you complete your tax return next April. Keep that in mind when you are spending your earnings!

Important rates to be aware of:

2012 Federal Income Tax

Net Income	Tax
$0 to $8,700	10%
Between $8,701 and $35,350	15%
Between $35,351 and $85,650	25%
Between $85,651 and $178,650	28%
Between $178,651 and $388,350,	33%
Over $388,350	35%
Source: Internal Revenue Service - 2012.	
(Single filing status only)	

2012 State Income Tax

State tax rates	
State	**Rate(s)/Income Level(s)**
Alabama	2% on income up to $500 4% on income up to $3,000 5% on income above $3,000
Alaska	No state tax
Arizona	2.59% on income up to $10,000 2.88% on income up to $25,000 3.36% on income up to $50,000 4.24% on income up to $150,000 4.54% on income above $150,000

Arkansas	1% on income up to $4,000
	2.5% on income up to $8,000
	3.5% on income up to $11,900
	4.5% on income up to $19,900
	6% on income up to $33,200
	7% on income above $33,200

California	1% on income up to $7,316
	2% on income up to $17,346
	4% on income up to $27,377
	6% on income up to $38,004
	8% on income up to $48,029
	9.3% on income up to $1,000,000
	10.3% on income above $1,000,000

| Colorado | 4.63% flat tax |

Connecticut	3% on income up to $10,000
	5% on income up to $50,000
	5.5% on income up to $100,000
	6% on income up to $200,000
	6.5% on income up to $250,000
	6.7% on income above $250,000

Delaware	0% on income up to $2,000
	2.2% on income up to $5,000
	3.9% on income up to $10,000
	4.8% on income up to $20,000
	5.2% on income up to $25,000
	5.55% on income up to $60,000
	6.75% on income above $60,000

District of Columbia	4% on income up to $10,000
	6% on income up to $40,000
	8.5% on income up to $350,000
	8.95% on income over $350,000

| Florida | No state tax |

Georgia	1% on income up to $750
	2% on income up to $2,250
	3% on income up to $3,750
	4% on income up to $5,250
	5% on income up to $7,000
	6% on income above $7,000

Hawaii	1.4% on income up to $2,400 3.2% on income up to $4,800 5.5% on income up to $9,600 6.4% on income up to $14,400 6.8% on income up to $19,200 7.2% on income up to $24,000 7.6% on income up to $36,000 7.9% on income up to $48,000 8.25% on income up to $150,000 9% on income up to $175,000 10% on income up to $200,000 11% on income above $200,000
Idaho	1.6% on income up to $1,380 3.6% on income up to $2,760 4.1% on income up to $4,140 5.1% on income up to $5,520 6.1% on income up to $6,900 7.1% on income up to $10,350 7.4% on income above $10,350
Illinois	5% flat tax
Indiana	3.4% flat tax
Iowa	0.36% on income up to $1,469 0.72% on income up to $2,938 2.43% on income up to $5,876 4.5% on income up to $13,221 6.12% on income up to $22,035 6.48% on income up to $29,380 6.8% on income up to $44,070 7.92% on income up to $66,105 8.98% on income above $66,105
Kansas	3.5% on income up to $15,000 6.25% on income up to $30,000 6.45% on income above $30,000
Kentucky	2% on income up to $3,000 3% on income up to $4,000 4% on income up to $5,000 5% on income up to $8,000 5.8% on income up to $75,000 6% on income above $75,000

Louisiana	2% on income up to $12,500 4% on income up to $50,000 6% on income above $50,000
Maine	2% on income up to $5,100 4.5% on income up to $10,150 7% on income up to $20,350 8.5% on income above $20,350
Maryland	2% on income up to $1,000 3% on income up to $2,000 4% on income up to $3,000 4.75% on income up to $100,000 5% on income up to $125,000 5.25% on income up to $150,000 5.5% on income up to $250,000 5.75% on income above $250,000
Massachusetts	5.3% flat tax
Michigan	4.35% flat tax
Minnesota	5.35% on income up to $23,670 7.05% on income up to $77,730 7.85% on income above $77,730
Mississippi	3% on income up to $5,000 4% on income up to $10,000 5% on income above $10,000
Missouri	1.5% on income up to $1,000 2% on income up to $2,000 2.5% on income up to $3,000 3% on income up to $4,000 3.5% on income up to $5,000 4% on income up to $6,000 4.5% on income up to $7,000 5% on income up to $8,000 5.5% on income up to $9,000 6% on income above $9,000
Montana	1% on income up to $2,700 2% on income up to $4,700 3% on income up to $7,200 4% on income up to $9,700 5% on income up to $12,500 6% on income up to $16,000 6.9% on income above $16,000

Nebraska	2.56% on income up to $2,400 3.57% on income up to $17,500 5.12% on income up to $27,000 6.84% on income above $27,000
Nevada	No state tax
New Hampshire	5% flat tax
New Jersey	1.4% on income up to $20,000 1.75% on income up to $35,000 3.5% on income up to $40,000 5.525% on income up to $75,000 6.37% on income up to $500,000 8.97% on income above $500,000
New Mexico	1.7% on income up to $5,500 3.2% on income up to $11,000 4.7% on income up to $16,000 4.9% on income above $16,000
New York	4% on income up to $8,000 4.5% on income up to $11,000 5.25% on income up to $13,000 5.9% on income up to $20,000 6.45% on income up to $75,000 6.65% on income up to $200,000 6.85% on income up to $1,000,000 8.82% on income above $1,000,000
North Carolina	6% on income up to $12,750 7% on income up to $60,000 7.75% on income above $60,000
North Dakota	1.51% on income up to $35,350 2.82% on income up to $85,650 3.13% on income up to $178,650 3.63% on income up to $388,350 3.99% on income above $388,350
Ohio	0.587% on income up to $5,100 1.174% on income up to $10,200 2.348% on income up to $15,350 2.935% on income up to $20,450 3.521% on income up to $40,850 4.109% on income up to $81,650 4.695% on income up to $102,100 5.451% on income up to $204,200 5.925% on income above $204,200

Oklahoma	0.5% on income up to $1,000
	1% on income up to $2,500
	2% on income up to $3,750
	3% on income up to $4,900
	4% on income up to $7,200
	5% on income up to $8,700
	5.25% on income above $8,700
Oregon	5% on income up to $3,150
	7% on income up to $7,950
	9% on income up to $125,000
	9.9% on income above $125,000
Pennsylvania	3.07% flat tax
Rhode Island	3.75% on income up to $57,150
	4.75% on income up to $129,900
	5.99% on income above $129,000
South Carolina	0% on income up to $2,800
	3% on income up to $5,600
	4% on income up to $8,400
	5% on income up to $11,200
	6% on income up to $14,000
	7% on income above $14,000
South Dakota	No state tax
Tennessee	6% flat tax
Texas	No state tax
Utah	5% flat tax
Vermont	3.55% on income up to $35,350
	6.8% on income up to $85,650
	7.8% on income up to $178,650
	8.8% on income up to $388,350
	8.95% on income above $388,350
Virginia	2% on income up to $3,000
	3% on income up to $5,000
	5% on income up to $17,000
	5.75% on income above $17,000
Washington	No state tax

West Virginia	3% on income up to $10,000 4% on income up to $25,000 4.5% on income up to $40,000 6% on income up to $60,000 6.5% on income above $60,000
Wisconsin	4.6% on income up to $10,570 6.15% on income up to $21,130 6.5% on income up to $158,500 6.75% on income up to $232,660 7.75% on income above $232,660
Wyoming	No state tax

How do these rates work?

For example, if you earned $130,000 per year in Maine, how much would you owe the federal and state governments in income taxes (excluding all deductions and adjustments)?

First, let's calculate the federal amount:

	Up to $8,700 at 10%	Between $8,701 and $35,350 at 15%	Between $35,351 and $85,650 at 25%	Over $85,651 to $178,650 at 28%
Calculation	8700 * 0.10	(35350 - 8700) * 0.15	(85650 - 35350) * 0.25	(130000 – 85650) * 0.28
Amount	$ 870.00 +	$ 3,997.50 +	$ 12,575.00 +	$ 12,418.00 =
Total Federal Tax	$29,860.50			

Now, let's calculate the state amount for Maine:

	Up to $5,100 at 2.0%	Between $5,101 and $10,150 at 4.5%	Between $10,151 and $20,350 at 7.0%	Over $20,350 at 8.5%
Calculation	5100 * 0.02	(10150-5100) * 0.045	(20350 - 10150) * 0.07	(130000 – 20350) * 0.085
Amount	$ 102.00 +	$ 227.25 +	$ 714.00 +	$ 9,320.25 =
Total State Tax	$10,363.35			

The total Federal and State (Maine) income tax for 2012 on $130,000 would be: $29,860.50 + $10,363.35 = **$40,223.85**

That's an average of almost 31% of your salary!!

And that is just the income tax. There are other deductions from your paycheck as well; including Social Security, Medicare, and any taxable benefits you may receive from your employer and so on.

Keep this in mind when you are creating a budget. Your salary and your "take home" pay are two totally different amounts.

✑ Exercise: Calculate the Tax

Now you try the previous example for yourself. Use the following tables to calculate the following federal and state income tax amounts:

1) $40,000 salary in Nevada

Federal:

	Up to $8,700 at 10%	Between $8,701 and $35,350 at 15%	Between $35,351 and $85,650 at 25%	Over $85,651 to $178,650 at 28%
Calculation				
Amount	$	$	$	$
Total Federal Tax	$			

State (Nevada):

Calculation			
Amount	$ +	$ +	$ +
Total State Tax	$		

2) $70,000 salary in Virginia

Federal:

	Up to $8,700 at 10%	Between $8,701 and $35,350 at 15%	Between $35,351 and $85,650 at 25%	Over $85,651 to $178,650 at 28%
Calculation				
Amount	$ +	$ +	$ +	$ =
Total Federal Tax	$			

State (Virginia):

	Up to $3,000 at 2%	Between $3,001 and $5,000 at 3%	Between $5,001 and $17,000 at 5%	Over $17,000 at 5.75%
Calculation				
Amount				
Total State Tax				

3) $27,000 salary in Massachusetts

Federal:

	Up to $8,700 at 10%	Between $8,701 and $35,350 at 15%	Between $35,351 and $85,650 at 25%	Over $85,651 to $178,650 at 28%
Calculation				
Amount				
Total Federal Tax	$			

State (Massachusetts):

Calculation			
Amount	$ +	$ +	$ +
Total State Tax	$		

Answers: See Appendix D

Current State Minimum Wage

Most states have their own minimum wage. Some states do not establish their own minimum wage so they use the federal rate. Each state that sets their own minimum wage does so independently of other jurisdictions. Therefore, one state government's increase to the minimum wage is no guarantee that other states will follow accordingly.

Jurisdiction	Minimum Wage (2012)
FLSA	$7.25
Alabama	None**
Alaska	$7.75
Arizona	$7.65
Arkansas	$6.25*
California	$8.00
Colorado	$7.64
Connecticut	$8.25
District of Columbia	$8.25
Florida	$7.67
Georgia	$5.15*
Illinois	$8.25

Louisiana	None**
Massachusetts	$8.00
Maine	$7.50
Michigan	$7.40
Minnesota	$6.15*
Mississippi	None**
Montana	$7.65
Nevada	$8.25
New Mexico	$7.50
Ohio	$7.70
Oregon	$8.80
Rhode Island	$7.40
South Carolina	None**
Tennessee	None**
Vermont	$8.46
Washington	$9.04

Wyoming $5.15*

*Where the state minimum wage is below the FLSA rate, the FLSA rate applies.
**Where the state has no legislated minimum wage, the FLSA rate applies.
Note: Where the state minimum wage is above the FLSA, the state rate applies.

Bank On It

Is your piggy-bank getting stuffed with cash? Nice! Now is the time to start thinking about opening a bank account. Let these tips help guide you when determining which type of bank account is right for you.

The Basics:

So why should you keep your money in a bank account? There are many reasons. Security is at the top of the list. Bank accounts hold your money for you and help you increase your savings by paying you interest. A bank account also enables you to pay your bills online, by check or at the bank in-person.

It is important to compare the different options available to you. The types of bank accounts include savings, checking and mixed:

- **Savings accounts**, as you can probably guess, help you save money! You can withdraw money when you want but they are really designed to help you hold on to your money and earn interest on it. Interest rates are usually very low (usually between 1% and 3% per year).

- **Checking accounts** are designed for purchasing and payment activities. They usually offer lower interest rates (if any) and higher transaction fees but allow you to write checks, pay bills online and email money transfers. Most banks will provide various plans that will charge you a single monthly fee for a specified number of transactions (for example, $9.95 per month for 3 checks plus one email transfer plus 10 ATM or online banking transactions).

- **Mixed accounts** are part savings and part checking. You can perform checking account transactions in addition to getting a certain interest rate to still encourage saving.

Exercise: Checking Plans: Which would you rather?

Which would you rather?

Review the following banking plans (columns 3 and 4) including the rates for individual transactions if you are not on a plan (column 2). Look at the average monthly usage proposed in the first column. Try to pick the best plan for the cost.

Your average monthly use	Bank Individual Rates	Plan 1	Plan 2
Debit card use (including ATM) averages 15 times/mo. Check use 2 times/mo. Email transfers 2 times/mo. Online banking payments 10 times/mo.	Debit card = $0.30 per use Checks = $0.50 each Email transfers = $1.50 per use Online bank transactions = $0.25 per use	$15.00/mo. Includes: 25 debit card uses 5 checks 4 email transfers 20 online banking (any uses above the plan allowed will be charged at the bank individual rates)	$7.95/mo. Includes: 30 debit card and/or online banking uses 2 checks per month 1 email transfer (any uses above the plan allowed will be charged at the bank individual rates)
	Average monthly total cost without a plan is $11.00	While this appears to be a good deal, your usage is not this high so this plan would be too expensive.	True cost: $7.95 plus overages: Email transfer: $1.50 + 5 Debit Card/Online at $1.50 = $10.95

While Plan 1 *appears* to be a good deal, it is not a good deal for you unless you plan on increasing your monthly transactions greatly. You won't be able to experience the savings that are intended for users of this plan. If you minimize your transactions where possible, Plan 2 may be the most economical, especially if you don't exceed the transactions allowed by the plan.

Check out the various plans available at your bank and determine which, if any, would be suitable for you now and which plan would be suitable a few years from now when you are living on your own.

If you already have a bank account, check your past few monthly statements or track your usage to see if your current plan (if any) is the best for you. Check with your bank to see if you can save money on a different plan.

♦ Tips:

- Before you choose a bank account, shop around to see what service fees each institution charges and the rates of interest that they pay. Some banks charge you for withdrawing money with your bank card, writing checks, paying bills online or getting service in-person from a teller at a bank branch.

- Save time by banking online. Online banking (or e-banking) is one of the most popular banking activities and it's not hard to see why. You can do almost all of your transactions online, from opening a new account and paying bills to investing in an Investment Retirement Account (IRA).

- Have money to invest? Talk to a professional financial planner. He or she can work with you to develop an investment plan that can help you save money and get ready for retirement (it may seem a long way away, but the earlier you start, the more money you'll have in the end). A Financial Planner will explain the different types of investments available to you and help you define your financial priorities. He / she can also assist you with investments that will minimize your taxes (see IRA further in this chapter).

- Do you have valuables that need protection, such as jewellery or legal documents? Most banks offer safe deposit boxes where, for a fee, you can store your valuables in a secure space in which only you and the bank have a key. The fees vary depending on the size of the box you rent. In some cases, this fee may be tax deductible.

Minimum Monthly Balance

Many institutions waive the monthly service fees on certain accounts if you maintain a minimum monthly balance in your account. Depending on the financial institution and the type of account, minimum balances range from $1,000 to $5,000. On most accounts, however, the minimum balance is generally $1,000 or $2,000.

Maintaining a minimum monthly balance can sometimes waive the monthly fee associated with your banking package. However, any cost savings should be compared to the returns or other opportunities you forego by keeping your money in your bank account (this concept is known as "opportunity cost"). For example, if you have a loan, it may be more cost-effective to pay it down than to keep the funds in your bank account to save the monthly service fees.

The following illustrations demonstrate that, when compared to conservative investment options (Certificates of Deposits ("CDs") or Government Issued Securities for example), you can save much more by maintaining the minimum monthly balance in your account, than you would earn if you invested the amount in a CD.

Let's look at some examples:

Example 1: : Basic Interest Rate Situation

Minimum Balance of $1,000

Mr. Franklin has a checking account at a bank where, if he maintains a minimum monthly balance of $1,000, his monthly fees of $6.50 are waived. As an alternative to keeping $1,000 or more in his account, Mr. Franklin could invest these funds in a one-year CD with an interest rate of 3%, compounded annually*.

compound interest is calculated on amount of original investment plus accumulated interest earned on prior periods. See "Principles of Saving" section for further details.

Annual savings from monthly minimum balance:	Return on a $1,000 investment in a CD:
$6.50 $\times$ 12 = $78	$30 or 3% (before income tax)
Return: $78 $\div$ $1,000 = 7.8% (after income tax)	

In the example above, it is to Mr. Franklin's advantage to maintain the minimum monthly balance in his account until he finds an investment with after-tax returns higher than 7.8%.

Example 2: High Interest Rate Situation

Minimum Balance of $5,000

Ms. Campbell has a checking account at a bank where, if she maintains a minimum monthly balance of $5,000, her monthly fees of $24.75 are waived. As an alternative to keeping $5,000 or more in her account, Ms. Campbell could invest these funds in a one-year CD, with an interest rate of 5%, compounded annually.

Annual savings from monthly minimum balance: $24.75 × 12 = $297 Return: $297 ÷ $5,000 = 5.94% (after income tax)	Return on a $5,000 investment in a CD: $250 or 5% (before income tax)

In the example above, it is to Ms. Campbell's advantage to maintain the minimum monthly balance in her account until she finds an investment with after-tax returns higher than 5.94%.

Example 3: Debt Situation

Minimum Balance of $2,000

Ms. Moffat has a checking account at a bank where, if she maintains a minimum monthly balance of $2,000, her monthly fees of $12.75 are waived. As an alternative to keeping $2,000 or more in her account, Ms. Moffat has a credit card debt of $2,000, with an annual interest rate of 28%, compounded annually.

Annual savings from monthly minimum balance: $12.75 \times 12 = 153 Return: $153 \div $2,000 = 7.65\%$ (after income tax)	Interest charged on a $2,000 credit card debt: $560 or 28% (after income tax)

In the example above, it is to Ms. Moffat's advantage to pay off the credit card debt as the savings from the minimum balance are not nearly enough to offset the interest charges that are incurring on the debt at a much higher rate.

Tips to Help You Save Money

- Shop around to determine the lowest-cost service package that best suits your needs. This is essential to saving money.

- If you choose a service plan that requires you to keep a minimum balance, make sure you maintain this balance *at all times*. Otherwise, you will be charged the full monthly fee.

- Use electronic and automated services (Internet, telephone, ATMs,) whenever possible. These usually cost less than in-person branch services.

- Use your own bank's ATMs as much as possible to avoid paying unnecessary fees. Banks tend to "double dip" when you withdraw from a rival's ATM by charging an additional fee (usually $1.50) each time for "processing" at the same time as the other bank is charging you a similar fee for the same transaction. This is a high surcharge ($3) especially if you withdraw only $20 (15%) or $40 (7.5%). This does not include your standard withdrawal fee from your bank.

- Try to minimize the number of transactions you make by withdrawing one larger amount instead of several smaller ones. However, be mindful, that when people withdraw larger sums at one time, they tend to spend it quicker and on items they normally wouldn't spend on just because they have the money available.

- In stores that allow it for free, withdraw cash from your account at the same time as you make a debit card purchase (in other words, add the amount you want to withdraw to your purchase and receive the cash as change).

- If a store wants to charge you a fee for a debit card purchase, use another means of payment such as a credit card or cash, or take your business elsewhere.

Saving for Success

"I have enough money to last me the rest
of my life, unless I buy something."
– Jackie Mason

Saving money is the foundation for financial success. For most people, saving money is not easy. Clearly, it is much easier to spend money than to save it. Since saving is not comfortable, it is something we must learn to do and continuously work at. Saving money over a lifetime requires a conscious effort and an ongoing focus so that it becomes a habit.

Are you a spender or a saver? Regardless of the answer, most of us could all use a little more savings so here are some principles for saving money.

1. **Know how much you make and how much you spend.**

    The starting point for any financial goal is to understand your spending patterns. Track your expenses. Just knowing how much you spend and where you spend your money sets the foundation for a sound financial future. (See the "Budgeting" section for guidance, later in this book.)

2. Save first, spend later.

Now is the time to get started. Start an automatic savings plan with your bank. Arrange to have money automatically come out of your bank account or off your paycheck. Most people spend first and try to save what little they have left over. The best plan is to save first and then spend what you have left over. Usually there are no fees for an automatic savings plan.

3. Understand the benefits of compound interest over simple interest.

There are two common types of interest – simple and compound. Compound interest occurs when interest is earned and it is added to the principal (i.e. original amount invested). Future interest is then earned on the principal and the past interest earned. The other option is simple interest where interest is *not* added to the principal. Future interest is earned on the principal only.

Compound interest is the type that will grow your money faster. The key to understanding compound interest is that once you get enough money working for you, you then no longer have to work for money.

How Interest Works

Here's an example of the difference between simple and compound interest on a savings account:

Simple Interest

Simple interest is calculated by multiplying the original deposit ("the principal" - e.g. $1000) by the interest rate (e.g. 5%) by the number of periods over the life of the deposit (e.g. 24 months).

For example, using the figures above, our $1000 principal would be at 5% per year, over a period of 2 years (as opposed to 24 months). The calculation would be 1000 x 0.05 x 2 (principal x interest x term) = 100. The amount of simple interest that we would receive on this principal over the two year term would be $100.

Compound Interest

Compound interest relates to charges the bank must pay not just on the original amount deposited, as in simple interest, but also on any interest earned in previous terms. To illustrate the difference between compounding interest and simple interest, consider the following very simplified scenario of a $1000 deposit invested at 10% over 2 years (assuming no withdrawals are taken until the end of the term):

Example of Simple vs. Compound Interest on a $1000 investment over 2 years

Simple Interest:

| 1st year | $ 1,000 | x | 1 year | x | 10% | = | $ 100 interest |
| 2nd year | $ 1,000 | x | 1 year | x | 10% | = | $ 100 interest |

Total   **Interest:**   **$ 200**

Total of the original loan amount plus interest =   **$ 1,200**

In this scenario, the total amount of interest paid over the 2 year period would be   **$200**

Compound Interest:

| 1st year | $ 1,000 | x | 1 year | x | 10% | = | $ 100 interest |
| 2nd year | $ 1,100 | x | 1 year | x | 10% | = | $ 110 interest |

Total   **Interest:**   **$ 210**

Total of the original investment amount plus interest =   **$ 1,210**

In this scenario, with interest compounded annually, the total amount of interest earned is **$210**

4. Start saving sooner than later.

The sooner you start saving, the more you will have later based on the compound interest example above. Don't procrastinate! It's never too late to start.

5. Something is better than nothing.

How much should you save? The amount is less important than getting a savings plan started soon. You've got to start the habit. Never let any hurdles get in the way of getting you started. Remember something is better than nothing and more is better than less.

6. Stay disciplined.

Saving money is hard work. It is so easy to get lured into spending your money on the next gadget. Saving money requires both effort and discipline. But the rewards are worth it!

How to Open a Bank Account

Now that you know about different types of bank accounts, you are ready to open an account of your own. Where can you do this and what documentation do you need? Firstly, before you go to your nearest bank branch, you should be aware of your rights.

What do you have to do to open an account?

To open an account, you have to go to the bank in-person, and show the bank some acceptable identification (I.D.). You must use **original** I.D., not a photocopy. As well, some banks require between $25 – $100 as an initial deposit to get the account started. If that is a problem, check around to find a bank that doesn't require this initial deposit.

What identification (I.D.) do you need?

Two pieces of ID, one of them must be **photo ID** (passport, drivers licence etc.). The other one can be a non-photo ID, like another bank card, social security card etc. If you don't have a Social Security Number, shop around and find a bank which doesn't require a SSN. There are lots of them.

Information you should receive when you open your account:

When you open an account, a bank should provide you with the following information preferably in **writing** (either at or before the time the account is opened):

- A copy of the account agreement.

- For an account that pays interest, the rate of interest on the account and how it will be calculated.

- All of the charges that apply to the account.

- How you will be notified of any increase in those charges, and of any new charges to the account.

- The bank's procedures if you have a complaint about any charges on your account.

- The bank's policies with respect to hold periods on deposits.

When can a bank refuse to open a personal bank account?

A bank can legitimately refuse to open a personal bank account for you if:

- The bank has reasonable grounds to believe that you'll use the account to break the law or commit fraud; and/or

- You've committed a crime or fraud against a financial institution during the past seven years; and/or

- It has reasonable grounds to believe that you intentionally provided false information when you opened the account; and/or

- It has reasonable grounds to believe that opening the account would expose its employees or customers to physical harm, harassment or abuse; and/or

- You do not agree to let the bank verify if the four circumstances mentioned above can apply to you and to verify the pieces of identification that you present to the bank; and/ or

- You can't provide acceptable identification.

- You previously closed an account that was overdrawn or wrote too many bounced checks.

- You show up as high risk in the ChexSystems database.

What is the ChexSystems?

ChexSystems is a database that banks use to determine if potential customers are too great of a risk to the bank. Banks will report you to this system if they close your account for negative balances or if you lied when you opened your account. Generally the bank will list the reason. The information can stay on the Chexsystems records for five years.

Some banks will not allow you to be a customer as long as you are on the list. Other banks will allow you to open an account if you have proof that you have paid off a balance that you owe the other bank. Some banks will offer you an account with higher fees, which help to offset the bank's risk for having a customer with previous mistakes.

You can request a report from ChexSystems if you have been denied an account in the last sixty days. You can ask the bank to give you information on how to receive a report or visit their www.consumerdebit.com. Once you receive the report you will need to clear up any fees that you owe other banks. When you clear up your debts that show up in the report, they will send in a report to the bank that the account has been paid. You can also request a letter stating this that you can take with you to the bank. You can dispute any information by contacting ChexSystems as well.

You can avoid being reported to ChexSystems by contacting your bank when you are in the negative. Some banks are willing to work with you as long as you are making a real and steady effort to bring your account back into the positive. This works the best if you communicate with your bank in person at the branch.

What if the bank wants to check your credit report?

When you ask to open a personal bank account, the bank often contacts a credit-reporting agency to get a copy of your credit report. Credit-reporting agencies are organizations that maintain credit reports for millions of American consumers. Banks can use your credit report to double-check the information you provide them. Your file will show and confirm to the bank information such as the following:

- Your personal identification (your name, address, birth date, etc.).
- Your employment history.
- Your current and past debts.
- Whether you pay your bills on time.
- Your bankruptcy history, and any judgments and/or third-party collections, if any.

Your file will also indicate to the bank any confirmed misuse or irregularities related to your address, social insurance number or telephone number.

This information will help the bank determine the reasons for refusal that apply to you. It will also help the bank decide what you can do with your account.

How the bank uses your credit information

The bank may use the information it obtains from the credit bureau check to help it decide what you can do with your personal bank account. The information will help the bank:

- Establish how much money you can withdraw from your account through an automated banking machine; and
- Determine whether you will be able to deposit checks at an automated banking machine and how long the bank will place a "hold" on the money you deposit into your account by check; and
- Decide whether to provide you with a checking account or a basic savings account.

Why the bank may reject your new account application

A bank may reject your application for a checking or savings account. If your credit report indicates you have a history of mishandling an account—perhaps you've bounced a lot of checks or done something to cause another financial institution to close one of your accounts —the bank may refuse to open an account for you. Note: If the bank declines your application based on information in a credit report, you must be told so and be given a chance to correct information in your report that may be inaccurate.

Your bank may close your deposit account and give you your money back. Examples of when that could happen:

- You bounce a certain number of checks.
- You refuse to pay the fees for bouncing checks (or some other fees, for that matter). Or,
- You don't make any deposits or withdrawals for many years and the bank's efforts to locate you prove unsuccessful, in which case the bank typically will transfer funds from these "dormant" accounts to the state government's unclaimed property office.

When can a bank deduct money from your account?

Your bank may deduct money from your account under certain circumstances without your consent. For example, you have an auto loan with the same bank where you have a checking account. If you don't make a monthly loan payment, the bank may be able to deduct the payment from your deposit account. The bank's right to divert money to cover a debt is governed by state law, which can vary significantly from state to state. If your bank has the right to take funds to cover money you owe the institution, this right is probably noted in your loan contract. Some state laws require the bank to give you advance notice before taking the loan payment; others don't.

What about online banks?

As use of the Internet continues to expand, more banks are using online services to offer products and services or otherwise enhance communications with consumers.

The Internet offers the potential for safe, convenient new ways to shop for financial services and conduct banking business, any day, any time. However, safe banking online involves making good choices – decisions that will help you avoid costly surprises or even scams.

Here are some tips from the FDIC:

1. Confirm that the online bank is legitimate:

   Read the "About Us' section on their website. You may find a brief history of the bank, the official name and address of the bank's headquarters, and information about its insurance coverage from the FDIC.

2. Protect yourself from fraudulent websites

For example, watch out for copycat Web sites that deliberately use a name or Web address very similar to, but not the same as, that of a real financial institution. The intent is to lure you into clicking onto their Web site and giving your personal information, such as your account number and password. Always check to see that you have typed the correct Web site address for your bank before conducting a transaction. And if you receive an email with a link, mouse over the link to see the true internet address that you would be going to if you clicked on it. Most banks will not send you messages to your email address.

3. Check the FDIC's database of FDIC-backed institutions at www.fdic.gov.

The FDIC ("Federal Deposit Insurance Corporation") is an independent agency of the federal government that insures your family's deposits up to $250,000 in all accounts against bank failures. The FDIC directly supervises more than 4,900 banks for operational safety and soundness. Also remember that not all banks operating on the Internet are insured by the FDIC. Many banks that are not FDIC-insured are chartered overseas. If you choose to use a bank chartered overseas, it is important for you to know that the FDIC may not insure your deposits. Check with your bank or the FDIC if you are not certain.

FDIC's Depositor Bill of Rights

You have the right to:

1. Automatic deposit insurance coverage when you open a deposit account at an FDIC-insured bank, with no additional action on your part.

2. Separate FDIC insurance coverage for deposits held at different FDIC-insured banks.

3. Confirm that a bank is insured by using the FDIC's Bank Find service (www.fdic.gov/bankfind) or by calling the FDIC toll-free at 1 (877) ASK-FDIC.

4. FDIC insurance coverage of at least $250,000 for your deposits at an FDIC-insured bank.

5. Deposit insurance coverage of more than $250,000 at a single bank when deposits are held in different "ownership categories," such as a single, joint and trust accounts.

6. Confirm that your deposits are within the insurance limits by using EDIE the Estimator at www.FDIC.gov/EDIE or by calling 1-877-ASK-FDIC.

7. Be informed when a financial product offered by your bank is not covered by FDIC insurance.

8. Prompt access to your insured deposits in the event your bank fails.

9. Receive distributions from the receivership if you are an uninsured depositor, as the sale of assets permits.

10. Sleep well, knowing that since the creation of the FDIC, no depositor has ever lost one penny of insured deposits.

Correcting Bank Errors

It is important to check your credit card account and bank account statements regularly. The Fair Credit Billing Act (FCBA) and Electronic Fund Transfers Act (EFTA) establish procedures for resolving mistakes on credit card account and bank account statements.

When most customers find a mistake on their bill, they pick up the telephone and call the company to correct the problem and feel that this action protects them. Telephoning on its own does not trigger the legal safeguards under the Fair Credit Billing Act. To be protected under the law, you must send <u>a separate written billing error notice</u>, to the financial institution. Your notice must reach the bank within 60 days after the first bill containing the error was mailed to you. The written notice must be sent to the address provided on the bill for billing error notices (and not, for example, directly to the store, unless the bill says that is where it should be sent). In your letter, you must include the following information:

- Your name and account number;

- A statement that you believe the bill contains a billing error and the dollar amount involved, and;

- The reason you believe there is a mistake.

The FCBA generally applies to "open end" credit accounts, such as credit cards or department store accounts. Many credit cards have an online process to submit your discrepancy complaint.

The EFTA applies to electronic fund transfers transactions involving automated teller machines (ATMs), debit cards, other point-of-sale debit transactions, and other electronic banking transactions that can result in the withdrawal of cash from your bank account.

Under the EFTA, if there is a mistake or unauthorized withdrawal from your bank account through the use of a debit card, you must notify your financial institution of the problem or error within 60 days after the statement containing the problem or error was sent. For retail purchases, your financial institution has up to 20 business days to investigate after receiving notice of the error.

You must notify your institution immediately upon learning that your debit card or credit card has been misplaced or lost. If you do not report the loss within two business days after you realize the card is missing, and if someone uses the card without your permission, you may lose from $50 to $500. If you do not report an unauthorized transfer or withdrawal within 60 days after your statement is sent to you, you risk unlimited loss.

Checklist - some things to think about

- What is more important to you: convenience or low fees?

- How do you like to do your banking? Do you want to make your banking transactions in-person only? (This is called in-branch banking.) Self-serve only? (by doing your banking through the automated teller/banking machines [ATMs/ABMs], phone or Internet)? Perhaps you need a combination of in-branch banking and self-serve banking.

- Where do you plan to do your banking? If you want to make some or all of your banking transactions in-person or at an ATM, are the bank branches or ATMs conveniently located so you can do the majority of your banking at that institution?

- There are extra fees you will have to pay if you do your banking transactions at the ATMs of another financial institution. Do you know what these extra charges are? Do you know the locations of the ATMs of your own financial institution? Get to know where they are so you can use these ATMs instead to avoid paying additional charges.

- If you want to do some in-branch transactions, do the branches have convenient business hours?

- Does your financial institution offer a low-fee or no-fee account?

- Could you benefit from a student or youth's service package with minimal or no fees?

- Does the financial institution have service packages that include *all* the types of transactions you will need? Transactions include withdrawing money from your account, transferring money from and into your account, writing checks, paying bills or using your debit card.

- Are specialized services (such as certified checks, money orders, bank drafts overdraft protection, check return, safe deposit box, traveller's checks) important to you? If so, it may be more beneficial to look for a service package that includes those services than to pay a fee each time you use them.

- To choose the right service package, you will have to figure out how many times you think you will need to make a withdrawal, a transfer, a bill payment, a direct payment or write a check, each month. How many transactions will your service package allow you to make each month? This is called the "monthly transaction limit". (See the exercise: "Checking Plans: Which Would You Rather?" earlier in the book.)

- If you go over this "monthly transaction limit", there may be a cost for each additional transaction you make. Do you know what you will have to pay for each additional transaction?

- Depending on your service package, sometimes the financial institution will not charge you the monthly fee, especially if you keep a specified minimum amount of money in your account. Do you know what the minimum amount would be so you can avoid paying this fee?

Payday Loans

What are payday loans?

Payday loans are paycheck cashing stores that charge a fee to cash your check. Payday lenders typically extend loans based on a percentage of your net pay (i.e. after taxes and deductions) until your next payday (generally within two weeks or less). You provide the payday lender with a post-dated check or authorize a direct withdrawal for the value of the loan plus any interest or fees charged.

Some payday lenders will cash your post-dated check or process the direct withdrawal on the due date of the loan. Others will require that you repay the loan in cash on or before the due date, and may charge an additional fee if the loan is not repaid on time. If there are insufficient funds in your account, you may also be required to pay a return fee to the payday lender and/or a non-sufficient funds (NSF) fee to his/her bank. In this instance, you may have the option of "rolling over" the loan – that is, taking out another payday loan to pay off the original loan – for an additional fee.

Pay day loan companies are under scrutiny for their excessive interest rates and fees. Regulation of the industry is handled primarily by individual states. Finance charges on payday loans are typically in the range of 15% to 30% of the amount for the two-week period, which translates to annual percentage rates (APRs) from 390% to 780%.

If you calculate the rate of interest charged on payday loan transactions using the definitions and methods specified in the Financial Code where exceeding 36% annual interest is not allowed, some payday loan companies appear to be charging criminal rates of interest. The following table illustrates this point by showing the details of an actual payday loan transaction.

Sample Payday Loan Transaction

Value of the payday loan advanced on 27 September 2009	$400.00
Amount paid by you on 14 October 2009	$451.28
Term of the loan	17 days
Breakdown of amount paid by you:	
Principal	$400.00
Interest	$8.64
Per item fee	$9.99
Check-cashing fees (7.99% of principal and interest)	$32.65
Effective annual rate of interest	1,242%

Consumer advocacy groups have raised concerns regarding what they view as the "predatory" lending practices of some payday lenders. While the federal and state governments are reviewing potential legislation to standardize the industry, the industry currently remains unregulated.

The following states have made payday loans illegal:

- Arizona
- Arkansas
- Connecticut
- Georgia
- Maine
- Maryland
- Massachusetts (not strictly illegal but highly regulated)
- New Hampshire
- New Jersey
- New York
- North Carolina

- Pennsylvania

- Vermont

- West Virginia

District of Columbia

The maximum interest rate that payday lenders may charge in the District of Columbia is 24 percent which is the same maximum interest rate for banks and credit unions. Payday lenders also must have a license from the District government in order to operate. As a result of the interest-rate cap enacted by D.C., all licensed payday lenders have withdrawn from the market, and no lawful payday loans are presently available in D.C.

New Mexico

New Mexico caps fees, restricts total loans by a consumer and prohibits immediate loan rollovers, in which a consumer takes out a new loan to pay off a previous loan. Once a loan is repaid, under the new law, the borrower must wait 10 days before obtaining another payday loan. The law caps fees at $15.50 for each $100 borrowed. A borrower's cumulative payday loans cannot exceed 25 percent of the individual's gross monthly income.

North Carolina

North Carolina negotiated agreements with all the payday lenders operating in the state. The state regulates that the last three lenders will stop making new loans, will collect only principal on existing loans and will pay $700,000 to non-profit organizations for relief.

Arizona

Arizona law prohibits lending institutions to charge greater than 36% annual interest on a loan. This caused many payday loan companies to shut down their Arizona operations.

Payday lenders claim they are the only option for debt-strapped consumers. But borrowing more money at triple-digit interest rates is never the right solution for people in debt. Instead, payday loans make problems worse. As research proves, virtually everyone takes more than one payday loan and thus the loans are similar to an addiction. This is not a legitimate loan product that benefits consumers. In fact, because most consumers believe they could be prosecuted for passing a bad check, the payday loan suddenly becomes their priority debt. Thus, the original debt problems that brought them to the lender often cannot be resolved.

Therefore, it is recommended that due to fees and interest rates, pay day lenders are an expensive choice and are not recommended as a regular means to obtain cash.

Investing in your Future

Once you have your money saved, what should you do with it? There are many different options that have different risk and rewards levels.

Standard Investments

Investment	Advantages	Disadvantages
Savings Bonds – Government bond that can be purchased online at TreasuryDirect. (A bond is a commitment to pay a specified interest rate.)	☑ Safest investment ☑ Smallest amounts (i.e. as low as $50) ☑ Rate of return known at time of purchase ☑ Can be cashed at any time with some interest paid, makes great emergency funds	☑ Interest is not as high as some other investments ☑ Interest is taxed ☑ Cannot be sold to other investors. ☑ Can no longer be bought through banks.

Savings account – a bank account that pays interest for saving money	☑ Safe, insured by government ☑ Pays interest ☑ Can deposit or withdraw money at any time ☑ Bank keeps record of amounts saved	☑ Interest rates are lower than other investments ☑ Interest is taxed ☑ Interest rates are not guaranteed, they fluctuate.
CD (Certificates of Deposit) – A certificate guaranteeing a fixed rate of interest on the money you deposit	☑ Safe, insured by government ☑ Higher interest than savings account ☑ Interest rate is same for 1-5 years	☑ Money must be left in for full period (usually 6 months-5 years) to get full rate of interest ☑ Interest is taxed ☑ Cannot be sold to another person ☑ May be penalty for withdrawing money early
Mutual Funds – A collection of different financial investments	☑ May be safer than buying stocks ☑ Mutual fund is overseen by experienced manager ☑ Allows diversification ☑ May reduce risk	☑ Market value goes up and down ☑ Future rate of return is uncertain ☑ There may be penalties if you withdraw your money early
Stocks – Part ownership of a company	☑ Potential for higher return on investment in market ☑ As an investor, you direct your money to a specific company of interest to you ☑ Can track the value of the investment daily on the Internet or newspaper	☑ Rate of return is uncertain ☑ May not be able to get cash from sale of stocks when needed ☑ Pay commission on trading ☑ Can be complex ☑ Many factors can impact stock values

Long Term Investment Plans

There are a few government programs that encourage specific savings that can provide tax benefits.

Program	Tax Benefits/Deferrals
IRA stands for **Investment Retirement Account**. An IRA is a government approved plan through which you save money for retirement. IRAs were designed to encourage and help Americans save for their retirement.	The contributions you make to a Traditional IRA are **tax deductible**, reducing your taxable income. Your IRA contributions offer a deferral of tax because the government allows you to push a portion of your taxable income to a future year such as when you retire when you are expected to be in a lower tax bracket. (Except in a Roth IRA where contributions are made after-tax so no tax is taken upon withdrawal unlike the Traditional IRA.) The income earned in an IRA is tax sheltered. This means that the investments inside your IRA will not be taxed as they grow each year. Over time, this significantly increases your earnings. Taxes on your Traditional IRA investments are not paid until you withdraw funds. Roth IRA's are made with after-tax cash so taxes are not paid when you withdraw the money. By that time you should be retired and your annual income may likely be much less and so will your tax rate. In both cases, you must start withdrawing from your IRA no later than the age of 70 ½.
401(k) is a type of investment retirement account established by employers who may contribute to their employee's account as a benefit.	Similar to the Traditional IRA, the contributions are tax deductible, reducing your taxable income. In some cases employers will match their contribution dollar-for-dollar up to a specific percentage of your salary. The contribution limits on 401(k)s are higher that IRAs. The one risk that you may want to consider with 401(k)s is that you should find out what your contributions are being invested in. It's not uncommon for a company to invest a large percentage of its 401(k) into its own stock. If the percentage is too high, you risk losing it all if the company shuts down. That is why you should balance your

	investments between a 401(k) and an IRA if you can afford to.
A **529 plan** is a tax-advantaged investment vehicle designed to encourage saving for the future higher education expenses of a designated beneficiary.	A 529 Plan is an education savings plan operated by a state or educational institution designed to help families set aside funds for future college costs. 529 Plans can be used to meet costs of qualified colleges nationwide. In most plans, your choice of school is not affected by the state your 529 savings plan is from. You can be a NY resident, invest in a CA plan and send your student to college in FL. 529 plans can differ from state to state. There are two types of 529 plans: prepaid or savings plans. **Savings Plans** work much like a 401K or IRA by investing your contributions in mutual funds or similar investments. The plan will offer you several investment options from which to choose. Your account will go up or down in value based on the performance of the particular option you select. **Prepaid Plans** let you pre-pay all or part of the costs of an public college education. Educational institutions can offer a 529 prepaid plan but not a 529 savings plan Although your contributions are not deductible on your federal tax return, your investment grows tax-deferred, and distributions to pay for the beneficiary's college costs come out federally tax-free. Your own state may offer some tax breaks as well in addition to the federal treatment. The amounts you can put in are substantial (over $300,000 per beneficiary in many state plans). Generally, there are no income limitations or age restrictions. Anyone can establish and contribute to a 529 plan on behalf of a designated beneficiary. This means that relatives, family, friends and even the designated beneficiary can establish the 529 plan for him- or herself.

A **Coverdell Education Savings Account** (also known as an **Education Savings Account**, a **Coverdell ESA**, a **Coverdell Account**, or just an **ESA**), is a tax-advantaged investment account designed to encourage savings to cover future education expenses	The tax treatment of Coverdell ESAs is much the same as that of 529 plans with a few important differences. Like a 529 plan, Coverdell ESAs allow money to grow tax deferred and proceeds to be withdrawn tax free for qualified education expenses at a qualified institution. However the definition of qualified expenses in an ESA includes primary and secondary school*, not just college and university. Coverdell ESAs have lower maximum contribution limits. 529 plans generally have no restrictions on contributions, up to the maximum lifetime contribution.
	Coverdell ESAs can allow almost any investment including stocks, bonds, and mutual funds, while 529 plans only allow a choice among a number of state run programs. The rules for investments allowed in ESAs are the same as those for IRAs.
	Balances in a Coverdell ESA must be disbursed on qualified education expenses by the time the beneficiary is 30 years old or given to another family member below the age of 30 in order to avoid taxes and penalties; there is no age limit for 529 plans.
	Coverdell ESAs allow withdrawing the money tax free for qualified elementary and secondary school expenses; 529 plans do not.
	The income level of a donor may affect contributions into a Coverdell ESA, but would not affect contributions to a Section 529 plan.
	*After Dec. 31, 2012, only postsecondary education expenses will qualify for the tax law; K-12 expenses will no longer be eligible.

Ways to Pay

The days of "cash only" are behind us. With so many different ways to pay for expenses available to us, it can be confusing as to which way is best. Here is a chart of the advantages and disadvantages of the most accepted types of payments.

Payment Methods

Payment Method	Advantages	Disadvantages
Cash – Paper currency and coins.	☑ Always accepted ☑ You know how much you have ☑ Tangible	☒ Can be easily stolen/lost ☒ Doesn't gain in value ☒ Not convenient to carry large amounts for large purchases (house, car, etc.)

Checks –

Financial instrument instructing a financial institution to pay a specific amount of a specific currency from a specific account held in the writer's name with that institution.

☑ You don't have to carry a wad of money so it is physically safe

☑ You can't spend more than you have in your account

☒ Not always accepted

☒ Need ID to use (hassle)

☒ Handwritten

☒ Signature can be forged

☒ No trust as you can't give someone a signed check to fill in amount

☒ Sometimes needs to be certified for large purchases so you need to go to the bank to use in this case

Debit Card –

Plastic card which provides an alternative payment method to cash when making purchases. Funds are withdrawn immediately from the owner's bank account.

☑ Convenient

☑ Safe (if you keep your PIN confidential)

☑ Can't spend more than you have in your account

☒ May forget your PIN

☒ Card can be lost

☒ Card can be demagnetized and needs replacement

☒ If ATM system down, you cannot access your money

☒ Bank and user fees for transactions

Credit Card –

Entitles its holder to buy goods and services based on the holder's promise to pay for these goods and services. They allow the consumers to maintain a balance, at the cost of having interest charged.

☑ Convenient

☑ Access to higher amounts

☑ Earn credit rating

☑ Buy now, pay later

☑ No transaction charges

☑ Some have reward point system

☒ Easy to overspend

☒ High interest rate

☒ Lose credit rating if you miss any payments

☒ Annual fees

☒ Potential for fraud

Electronic Funds Transfer (EFT) –

Transfer of money electronically through your online banking account to pay bills online.

☑ Convenient

☑ Transfer money immediately

☑ Safe, little security risk

☑ No transaction charges

☑ Private

☑ Online record of transaction

☒ Must have access to internet

☒ There may be a delay of several days before bill is actually paid

☒ There may be a monthly charge for internet access

☒ Have to keep password secret

Stored value Cards / Gift Cards –

Issued by retailers or banks to be used as an alternative to a non-monetary gift.

☑ Gives a bonus for each transaction

☑ No cost

☒ Must use at the issuing business

☒ May be hard to claim rewards

☒ Potential loss of privacy

☒ Not secure

☒ Card can be lost

Exercise: Which should you use?

Which version of payment should you use? (Select the best method. In some cases, there may be more than one option.)

Buying gum and milk at the convenience store.	Cash? Check? Debit Card? Credit Card? EFT?
Taking your best friend out to dinner for his/her birthday.	Cash? Check? Debit Card? Credit Card? EFT?
Buying groceries for the week.	Cash? Check? Debit Card? Credit Card? EFT?
Buying gas.	Cash? Check? Debit Card? Credit Card? EFT?

Paying the hydro bill.	Cash? Check? Debit Card? Credit Card? EFT?
Making a donation to charity.	Cash? Check? Debit Card? Credit Card? EFT?
Paying your rent.	Cash? Check? Debit Card? Credit Card? EFT?
Getting your car washed at the annual charity car wash.	Cash? Check? Debit Card? Credit Card? EFT?
Going to McDonald's.	Cash? Check? Debit Card? Credit Card? EFT?
Buying an iPod.	Cash? Check? Debit Card? Credit Card? EFT?

See Appendix D for answers.

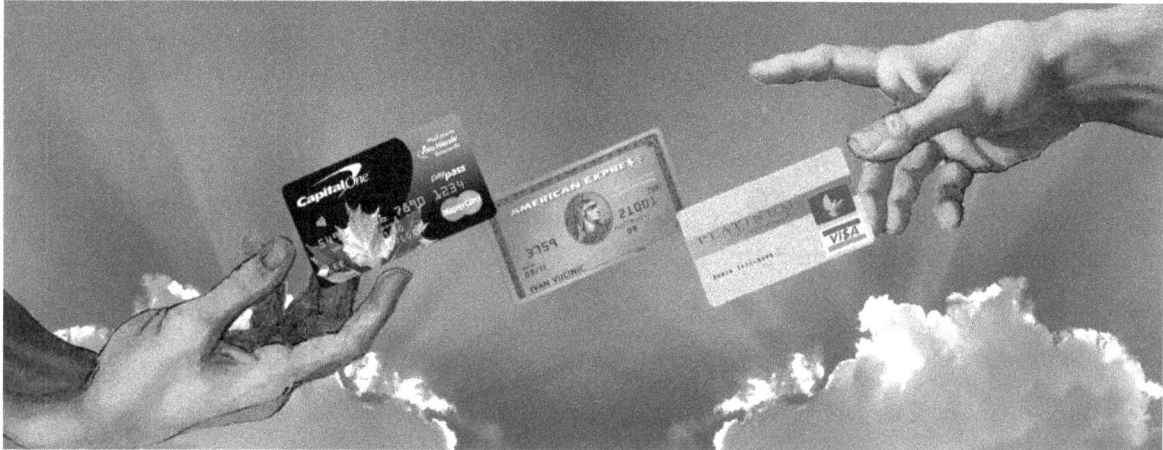

Give Credit Cards Where Credit is Due

Shopping for the Best Credit Card

In addition to looking at fees and interest (also known as the annual percentage rate or "APR") that you will be charged, consider your lifestyle and past payment history when shopping for a credit card. Factors you may want to consider include:

- A fixed (i.e. set-in-stone) vs. a variable rate of interest. Most cards use a variable rate which can change monthly depending on the prime rate issued by each bank. A fixed rate will not fluctuate as the prime rate changes (although a credit card company reserves the right to change their rate with notice to its customers).

- The minimum payment that you are required to make.

- The maximum amount that you can borrow without being penalized with an over-the-limit fee.

- Fees such as an annual fee, late payment charges and interest rates on cash advances.

- Circumstances when the credit card company can change the conditions of your agreement. Sometimes a credit card company will send you a multi-page pamphlet of fine print notifying you of numerous changes to their agreement with you. Some changes may include days you have to pay without interest penalties, changes in the reward plan, or changes in how interest is calculated. Their obligation is to notify you. They do not need to receive your consent or acknowledgement of receipt to proceed with the changes. These changes are rarely to your benefit.

- How the company calculates the finance charge. Is it based on the average daily balance, the balance at the beginning of the billing cycle, or another amount?

- A low introductory interest rate, if offered. When is the rate likely to increase? What is the new rate likely to be?

- Incentives such as cash rebates on purchases, purchase protection and frequent flyer miles.

- Your prior payment history. If you typically pay off your balance every month, the APR may be less of an issue than getting cash back with a purchase.

Credit Card Statements

Understanding your credit card statement is imperative if you regularly spend on your credit card and need to follow a tight budget. To many people, reading a credit card statement is fairly straightforward, yet for newcomers there may be a couple of features that need to be clarified. The key features of your credit card statement include:

		3			**9**	
Previous Balance		3	$815.33	Credit Limit	9	$18,250.00
LESS Payments & Credits		5	$300.00	Available Credit Limit		$17,259.91
PLUS New Charges/Adjustments inc. Interest, if any			$474.76	Available Cash Limit		$3,650.00
EQUALS New Balance		10	$990.09			

Payment Period Remaining

Minimum Amount Due on Sep 30, 2010   **2** $30.00   If each month you pay the Minimum Amount Due only   7 Year(s) 2 Month(s)

Statement includes payments and charges received by Sep 9, 2010   **4**

Your Transactions

Transaction Date	Posting Date	Details		Amount ($)
Aug 18	Aug 18	PAYMENT RECEIVED - THANK YOU Reference AT102300005000010009231	5	-300.00
Total of Payment Activity				**-300.00**
Aug 26	Aug 27	IFAW INC		5.00
Total of new transactions			8	**5.00**
Aug 9	Aug 11	TORONTO PARKING AUTH		12.00
Aug 10	Aug 11	RBC GENERAL		195.82
Aug 13	Aug 14	CLARKE HUSKY		58.50
Aug 17	Aug 18	PETSMART		38.39
Aug 23	Aug 25	AMAZON.COM		62.14
Aug 29	Aug 30	COSTCO		96.40
Total of new transactions				**463.25**

Transaction Date	Posting Date	Details		Amount ($)
OTHER ACCOUNT TRANSACTIONS				
Sep 9	Sep 9	INTEREST	6	6.51
Total of other account transactions				**6.51**

Account Number		3733 **XXXX XXX**
New Balance	**10**	$990.09
Minimum Due	**4**	$30.00
Payment Due Date		Sep 30, 2010

Amount Paid ($)

Category		Daily Periodic Rate 31 Billing days this Period	Interest	Current Annual Interest Rate	Annual Interest Rates		
					Preferred	Standard	Basic
Purchases	*12*	0.0356%	$6.51	12.99%	12.99 %	21.99 %	25.99 %
Funds Advance	*11*	0.0548%	$0.00	19.99%	19.99 %	21.99 %	25.99 %
Amex Cheques/Balance Transfers		0.0356%	$0.00	12.99%	12.99 %	21.99 %	25.99 %
			$6.51				

#1 – The Statement Period

Knowing this period of time is important to take advantage of your "interest free" period (the time span between transaction date and the payment due date which can be up to 55 days). So if you know that your statement date is always on the 9th of a month, it is advantageous to you to delay a purchase to the 10th or 11th of the month to get the maximum interest free period. These later purchases won't show up until the statement for the following month and therefore won't be included in your current card balance due.

Sometimes banks will promote a 55 day interest free period. It is misleading as it meant to give you the erroneous impression that all your purchases are eligible for 55 days of no interest. So when does the 55 day interest free period actually apply? What it actually applies to is the '55 days' from the start of your last statement period, till it's 'Payment due date' (**2**). From the statement above, this is a grace period of 53 days between the 27th of February and the 20th of April. If you made a purchase on April 16th for example, you only effectively have 4 interest free days on your purchase.

#2 – Payment Due Date

This is the date you must pay at least the 'minimum amount due' (**3**) for your current credit card statement. If you do not pay at least the minimum repayment, your credit card rating will be affected and you will be charged a late payment fee (usually around $10-40 depending on your bank).

#3 – Previous Balance

This is the amount that was not paid from the previous month's statement. You will be incurring interest on this amount daily until it is paid off.

#4 – Minimum Amount Due & Due Date

The Minimum Amount Due is also known as your "minimum repayment". This figure is often 2 - 5% of your balance or $10 - 30, generally whichever is higher applies. Try to avoid paying only the minimum repayment unless absolutely necessary, as it can take years to pay off balances as low as $500 (thus accumulating significant interest over that period of time).

The due date is very important to understand. If you don't make even the minimum payment by this date, you will risk your credit card being rejected for future purchases and your credit rating being negatively affected.

#5 – Payments/Refunds

This is the total amount of all your repayments made towards your credit card in your statement period to date.

#6 – Interest Charges

This is the amount of interest that you have been charged on your outstanding balance from your previous statement. Any time that you do not pay your balance in full on time, you will accumulate interest charges at the specified daily rate. These amounts can add up substantially so you should try to pay off as much of your credit card balance each month as you can realistically afford.

#7 – Rewards Program Earning (not available in the example above)

Many credit cards include "rewards" or "loyalty" programs such as flight miles, cash back, Amazon.com dollars, and so on. These programs are built into the card features as an enticement for you to use that card. This section shows you how many "points" you have earned towards that program.

#8 – Transactions

This area lists all your transactions, including the date of purchase, transaction reference code, what was purchased and how much it cost. Make sure that you review this thoroughly for charges that you did not make. If you find such charges, contact the credit card company within 30 days to file a complaint. If you act after 30 days, the credit card company may refuse to process the investigation. Check with your credit card company on what their policy and procedure is in this situation. Most companies will have this information posted on their website somewhere (usually under the section on how to file a dispute).

#9 – Credit Limit & Credit Available.

The credit limit is the maximum amount that you are allowed to charge to your card. If you exceed this amount, you will be charged a substantial penalty and your card may be disabled. The limit is comprised of overdue balances, new purchases, interest charges and penalties.

The credit available is the result of your credit limit minus your outstanding balance. It indicates how much credit is available before you reach your credit limit.

#10 – Account Balance

How much you currently owe on your credit card. If you have put more money on your card than your balance, this figure will be displayed as negative.

#11 – Purchase / Cash Advance Rate

These are your standard annual percentage rates (APR) on purchases and cash advances (i.e. cash withdrawals).

#12 – Daily Rate

Although interest rates are given as a yearly figure, this is the real figure which applies to your transactions. This is how much interest will accumulate on your purchases/cash advances each day. You can find this figure by dividing your annual rate by 365.

Key Credit Card Terms

If you don't understand the language, credit card offers and statements could lead you into deep debt -- or at least frantic frustration. For the clarification on the fine print, here's what these frequently used credit card terms mean.

Average daily balance

This is the method by which most credit cards calculate your payment due. An average daily balance is determined by adding each day's balance and then dividing that total by the number of days in a billing cycle.

For example:

Let's say throughout the month, your balances are:

Dates of the month	Balance
1st to 10th inclusive (10 days)	$100.00
11th to 19th inclusive (9 days)	$250.00
20th to 25th inclusive (6 days)	$200.00
26th to 31st inclusive (6 days)	$400.00

If you average totals for each day over the month (i.e. $100 x 10 + $250 x 9 + $200 x 6 + $400 x 6 = $6850.00 divided by 31 days), the average daily balance is $220.97.

The average daily balance is then multiplied by a card's monthly rate, which is calculated by dividing the annual percentage rate by 12.

For example, a card with an annual rate of 18 percent would have a monthly periodic rate of 1.5 percent (18% divided by 12 equals 1.5%). If that card had a $500 average daily balance it would yield a monthly finance charge of $7.50 (1.5% x $500 = 7.50).

In our example above, the monthly charge would be $3.31 ($220.97 x 1.5%).

✍ Exercise: Monthly Charges

Try to figure out what the monthly charge would be based an *annual* interest rate of 28% on the following figures: (see Appendix D for the answer.)

Dates of the month	Balance
1st to 7th inclusive (7 days)	$ 500.00
8th to 14th inclusive (7 days)	$ 750.00
15th to 22nd inclusive (8 days)	$ 900.00
23rd to 31st inclusive (9 days)	$1,400.00

Annual Percentage Rate (APR)

A yearly rate of interest that banks charge to advance / loan money to clients whether you are borrowing cash (loans or cash advance on your credit card), charging items on a credit card, financing a car or getting a mortgage.

Balance Transfer

The process of moving an unpaid credit card debt from one card to another. Credit card companies sometimes offer "teaser" rates to encourage its customers to move the balances that they may have on other cards to their credit card at a lower rate for a specified period of time. For example, you may receive a letter or credit card "checks" that give you a substantially lower rate (e.g. 2.99%) for six months if you transfer any outstanding amounts from any other credit card accounts. These can be advantageous as long as you understand how long the rate will last, what the rate will increase to after the specified term and if there is a service fee to make the transfer.

Cash-Advance Fee

A fee charged by the bank for using credit cards to obtain cash. This fee can be a flat per-transaction fee (e.g. $5 per withdrawal) or a percentage of the amount of the cash advance. For example, the fee may be expressed as follows: "2% / $10". This means that the cash advance fee will be either the greater of 2% of the cash advance amount or $10, whichever is higher.

The banks may limit the fee that can be charged to a specific dollar amount. The cost of a cash advance is also higher because there is generally no grace period. Interest starts being calculated from the moment the money is withdrawn.

Cardholder Agreement

The written statement that gives the terms and conditions of a credit card account. It must include the Annual Percentage Rate, the monthly minimum payment formula, annual fee if applicable, and the cardholder's rights in billing disputes. Changes in the cardholder agreement may be made, with advance written notice, at any time by the issuer.

Finance Charge

The fee for using a credit card is comprised of interest costs and other fees.

Grace Period

If the credit card user does not carry a balance, the grace period is the interest-free time a lender allows between the transaction date and the billing date. The standard grace period is usually between 20 and 30 days. If there is no grace period, finance charges will accumulate the moment a purchase is made with the credit card. People who carry a balance on their credit cards have no grace period.

Minimum Payment

The minimum amount a cardholder can pay to keep the account from going into default (i.e. your card is cancelled, collection agencies harass you and your credit rating is negatively affected). Some card issuers will set a high minimum if they are uncertain of the cardholder's ability to pay. Most card issuers require a minimum payment of two percent of the outstanding balance.

Over-The-Limit Fee

A fee charged for exceeding the credit limit on the card. So, if your credit limit is $5,000 and your balance creeps to $5,100, you will be charged a sizable penalty that will build until you lower your balance. In this case, a business may reject (or even cut up) your card during your transaction which can be both inconvenient and humiliating.

Periodic Rate

The interest rate described in relation to a specific amount of time. The monthly periodic rate, for example, is the interest charged per month; the daily periodic rate is the cost of interest charged per day.

Pre-Approved

A "pre-approved" credit card offer suggests that a potential customer has passed a preliminary credit-information screening. A credit card company can reject the customers it has invited with "pre-approved" junk mail if it doesn't like the applicant's credit rating.

Secured Card

It is a credit card that a cardholder guarantees with a savings account as a backup to ensure payment of the outstanding balance if the cardholder defaults on payments. It is used by people new to credit, or people trying to rebuild their poor credit ratings.

Teaser Rate

Often called the introductory rate, it is the below-market interest rate offered to entice customers to switch credit cards. For example, you may get mail encouraging you to transfer your balances from your other credit cards at a low rate of 2.99% for 10 months.

Variable Interest Rate

Percentage that a credit card owner or loan borrower pays for the use of money. The rate moves up or down periodically based on changes in other interest rates such as the Bank of Canada rate and/or bank interest rates.

Quiz: (courtesy of FCAC)

1. Last month, your credit card balance was zero. This month, your statement shows that you made a $500 purchase. If you can pay off only $400 by the due date indicated on your statement, you will be charged interest only on the $100 left to pay. True or False?

2. You make a purchase on your new credit card at the beginning of the month. Mid-month, you request a balance transfer - at a low promotional rate - from other credit cards to your new one. When you make a credit card payment, this payment is first applied to your purchase, since it occurred before the balance transfer. True or False?

3. All credit card issuers have the same rule: if you pay off your credit card bill in full by the due date indicated on your statement, you won't be charged interest on any purchases that appear on that statement. True or False?

4. You won't pay interest on a cash advance as long as you pay your credit card bill in full by the due date indicated on your statement. True or False?

5. All credit cards have the same grace period. True or False?

6. Most credit card issuers have formal policies in place to protect cardholders against unauthorized transactions on their accounts. True or False?

7. If you frequently pay your credit card just a couple of days after the due date, this won't affect your credit rating. True or False?

8. Credit rating agencies will charge you a fee for sending you a copy of your credit report by mail. True or False?

9. Your January statement, dated January 31, shows that you owe $550 because of a purchase you've been carrying over since October. Your next credit card payment is due on February 15. If you pay $550 on February 13, you won't owe anything more. True or False?

10. A credit card issuer can increase the administration fee it charges for a cash advance without telling you in advance. True or False?

(see the next page for the answers)

Answers:

1 –False - It is a common myth to think that you will pay interest only on the amount left to pay (also called the outstanding amount) on your credit card bill. If you don't pay in full by the due date indicated on your credit card statement, you lose the interest-free period on your new purchases, and:

You will be charged interest on the $400 you paid off - from the transaction date (or from the posted date) until the day you made the $400 payment; and

You will be charged interest on the $100 outstanding - from the transaction date (or the posted date) until the date you pay this amount in full.

2 – False - When you make a payment, it is usually applied first to the transaction with the lowest interest rate, regardless of whether there are older transactions in the account. The result is that you are usually left with the higher interest debt (the purchases). Your credit card agreement normally indicates the "order of transactions" that is followed by your credit issuer in applying payments.

3 – False - Not all credit card issuers are the same! With most of them, you will not be charged interest on purchases you made during the month if you pay in full and on time. But with some credit cards, if you haven't repaid every penny from your previous bill, you'll be charged interest not only on the amount outstanding, but also on any new purchases made, regardless of whether you pay those purchases in full. In other words, you lose your interest-free period on new purchases because you haven't paid the previous month's bill in full.

4. – False - Cash advances do not benefit from the interest-free period (only purchases do). In other words, you must pay interest on cash advances from the day you obtain them until you pay them off in full.

5. – False - Grace periods vary from card to card. They can range from 15 days to 60 days (charge cards). Check your credit card agreement to find out what grace period you have on your credit card.

6. -- True - Visa, MasterCard, and American Express have what they call "Zero-liability policies" that protect their cardholders from unauthorized transactions. If you find an unauthorized transaction on your account, let your credit card issuer know immediately.

They will investigate the matter and reimburse you in most cases provided that you file the complaint following their procedures within the amount of time that they specify (for example, within 60 days of the date of the unauthorized transaction).

7. -- False - Each month, your credit card issuer reports to the credit rating agencies whether you are paying on time. If you are late in making credit card payments, it will reflect negatively on your credit history and could seriously affect your credit rating. A tarnished credit rating could make it hard for you to get credit in the future and you might end up paying a higher interest rate on loans you do obtain.

8. -- False - If you request it be sent to you by mail, a copy of your credit report is free of charge from the major credit rating agencies (Equifax, Experian and TransUnion). You should obtain a copy of your credit report each year to ensure its accuracy (this does not affect your credit rating in any way). You may be charged a small fee for a more detailed report.

Warning: Only one website is authorized to fill orders for the free annual credit report you are entitled to under law — annualcreditreport.com. Other websites that claim to offer "free credit reports," "free credit scores" or " free credit monitoring" are not part of the legally mandated free annual credit report program. In some cases, the "free" product comes with strings attached. For example, some sites sign you up for a supposedly "free" service that converts to one you have to pay for after a trial period. If you don't cancel during the trial period, you may be unwittingly agreeing to let the company start charging fees to your credit card.

Some "imposter" sites use terms like "free report" in their names; others have URLs that purposely misspell annualcreditreport.com in the hope that you will mistype the name of the official site. Some of these "imposter" sites direct you to other sites that try to sell you something or collect your personal information.

9. -- False - Since you've been carrying a balance since October, you owe interest on that amount until the day you pay it off in full. If you wait until February 13 to make a payment, you will still owe interest that accrued between the dates of January 31 (your statement date) and February 13 (your payment date). This interest charge will appear on your February statement.

10. -- False - A credit issuer must give at least 45 days notice (and apply it to transactions occurring just 14 days after sending the notice) before it can make the following changes to your credit card agreement (this list is not exhaustive):

- Increase in fees for various transactions.

- Change in your fixed interest rate.

- Decrease in the grace period.

- Increase or decrease in the minimum payment.

If your credit card company is going to make changes to the terms of your card, it must give you the option to cancel the card before certain fee increases take effect. If you take that option, however, your credit card company may close your account and increase your monthly payment, subject to certain limitations.

For example, they can require you to pay the balance off in five years, or they can double the percentage of your balance used to calculate your minimum payment (which will result in faster repayment than under the terms of your account).

The company does **not** have to send you a 45-day advance notice if:

- you have a variable interest rate tied to an index; if the index goes up, the company does not have to provide notice before your rate goes up;

- your introductory rate expires and reverts to the previously disclosed "go-to" rate;

- your rate increases because you are in a workout agreement and you haven't made your payments as agreed.

Other rules regarding rates, fees and limits

- No interest rate increases for the first year. Your credit card company cannot increase your rate for the first 12 months after you open an account. There are some exceptions:

  - If your card has a variable interest rate tied to an index; your rate can go up whenever the index goes up.

  - If there is an introductory rate, it must be in place for at least 6 months; after that your rate can revert to the "go-to" rate the company disclosed when you got the card.

  - If you are more than 60 days late in paying your bill, your rate can go up.

  - If you are in a workout agreement and you don't make your payments as agreed, your rate can go up.

- Increased rates apply only to new charges. If your credit card company does raise your interest rate after the first year, the new rate will apply only to new charges you make. If you have a balance, your old interest rate will apply to that balance.

- Restrictions on over-the-limit transactions. You must tell your credit card company that you want it to allow transactions that will take you over your credit limit. Otherwise, if a transaction would take you over your limit, it may be turned down. If you do not opt-in to over-the-limit transactions and your credit card company allows one to go through, it cannot charge you an over-the-limit fee.

  If you opt-in to allowing transactions that take you over your credit limit, your credit card company can impose only one fee per billing cycle. You can revoke your opt-in at any time.

- Caps on high-fee cards. If your credit card company requires you to pay fees (such as an annual fee or application fee), those fees cannot total more than 25% of the initial credit limit. For example, if your initial credit limit is $500, the fees for the first year cannot be more than $125. This limit does not apply to penalty fees, such as penalties for late payments.

- Protections for underage consumers. If you are under 21, you will need to show that you are able to make payments, or you will need a co-signer, in order to open a credit card account. If you are under age 21 and have a card with a co-signer and want an increase in the credit limit, your co-signer must agree in writing to the increase.

- Standard payment dates and times. Your credit card company must mail or deliver your credit card bill at least 21 days before your payment is due. In addition:
  - Your due date should be the same date each month (for example, your payment is always due on the 15th or always due on the last day of the month).
  - The payment cut-off time cannot be earlier than 5 p.m. on the due date.
  - If your payment due date is on a weekend or holiday (when the company does not process payments), you will have until the following business day to pay. (For example, if the due date is Sunday the 15th, your payment will be on time if it is received by Monday the 16th before 5 p.m.).

- Payments directed to highest interest balances first. If you make more than the minimum payment on your credit card bill, your credit card company must apply the excess amount to the balance with the highest interest rate. There is an exception:

  > If you made a purchase under a deferred interest plan (for example, "no interest if paid in full by March 2012"), the credit card company may let you choose to apply extra amounts to the deferred interest balance before other balances. Otherwise, for two billing cycles prior to the end of the deferred

interest period, the credit card company must apply your entire payment to the deferred interest-rate balance first.

- No two-cycle (double-cycle) billing. Credit card companies can only impose interest charges on balances in the current billing cycle.

Credit and Debit Card Security

Using cards to pay for stuff is very convenient. Unfortunately, in the wrong hands, your cards can be used to steal your money. Do you know how to protect yourself? It is important to understand that you may be held responsible for losses if you are negligent with your cards.

The Basics:

- Keep your cards in a safe place and never leave them unattended.

- When using your chip credit card or debit card ensure that your personal identification number (PIN) is hidden and no one is looking over your shoulder to get it.

- Choose a PIN that does not contain obvious information that can be linked to you, such as your phone number or your birthday. Never disclose your PIN number, even to friends.

- Before sending your personal information (address, phone number, credit card number) over the Internet, always make sure that the website you're providing information to uses encryption to keep your data secure. There should be a padlock symbol in the bottom right corner of your web browser. As well, the end of the secure URL includes "Shtml".

- Keep track of the transactions on your debit and credit card accounts. With many accounts, you can retrieve your account information online. Call your bank or credit card company immediately if you suspect that someone else is purchasing things with your card.

- Before throwing away documents containing your personal information (e.g. credit card receipts, financial statements, old credit and debit cards, tax forms, computer storage devices, etc.), destroy them (cut up, shred, erase).

Can't I Just Pay the Monthly Minimum?

Your monthly credit card bill should include information on how long it will take you to pay off your balance if you only make minimum payments. It will also tell you how much you would need to pay each month in order to pay off your balance in three years. For example, suppose you owe $3,000 and your interest rate is 14.4%--your bill might look like this:

New balance	$3,000.00
Minimum payment due	$90.00
Payment due date	4/20/12

Late Payment Warning: If we do not receive your minimum payment by the date listed above, you may have to pay a $35 late fee and your APRs may be increased up to the Penalty APR of 28.99%.

Minimum Payment Warning: If you make only the minimum payment each period, you will pay more in interest and it will take you longer to pay off your balance. For example:

If you make no additional charges using this card and each month you pay. . .	You will pay off the balance shown on this statement in about. . .	And you will end up paying an estimated total of. . .
Only the minimum payment	11 years	$4,745
$103	3 years	$3,712 (Savings = $1,033)

Another example:

A card with a $1,500 balance and an APR of 18% will make a big difference to your debt with only $10 more per month on top of the $37 per month monthly minimum payment.

If you make no additional charges using this card and each month you pay. . .	You will pay off the balance shown on this statement in about. . .	And you will end up paying an estimated total of. . .
Only the minimum payment	13 1/3 years	$3,292
$103	3 2/3 years	$2,055 (Savings = $1,237)

Quiz:

The following true or false questions may help you learn more about credit card fraud.

1. If your credit card is lost, stolen or used without your permission, you should report this information right away to the credit card company. True or False?

2. Credit card issuers do not permit you to lend your credit card. Lending your card may void the consumer protections you have under laws and voluntary codes. True or False?

3. If you request an additional card for a family member, you are liable for all debt that person incurs. True or False?

4. There is no need to shred an empty (i.e. not filled out) or incomplete credit card application that came in the mail if you are just throwing it in the garbage. True or False?

Answers:

1. *True*
2. *True*
3. *True*
4. *False*

Credit Decisions

In a perfect world, you would never need to borrow money. Still, most people will eventually need a loan of some kind whether it is for tuition, a car loan, mortgage, etc. Credit, if used wisely, can be used to your advantage. The key is to know your borrowing options and avoid borrowing more than you need.

The Basics:

- There are lots of reasons to borrow money, such as paying for education, buying a house or car, paying for major purchases over time, making investments or using a line of credit or credit card when your cash flow is low.

- Borrowing money can be a useful tool for building your assets. For example, education can help you to get a better paying job, while buying a house gives you a place to live and a long term valuable asset. However, borrowing to buy gadgets, such as an iPod, PS3 or 3DTV, can become a major drain on your finances especially if you have to pay a high rate of interest.

- Before applying for a loan or credit card, shop around for the best interest rates and payment terms. Thorough research now could save you a lot of money later.

- Read the fine print on your loan or credit card agreement before you sign it! Knowing the terms and conditions in advance could save you a lot of money and grief later on.

- Beware of "payday" loans, which are small loans that a borrower usually is required to pay back on or before his or her next payday. These loans are one of the most expensive ways for a consumer to borrow money.

- Credit agencies keep track of your credit history - how much you have borrowed in the past and whether you have paid it back. If you have ever taken out a loan, used a credit card, signed up for utilities such as hydro, water or cable television, you will have a credit history. Your credit history is used by banks and businesses to decide whether to lend you money and how much interest to charge you.

- If you're having trouble getting credit or are suddenly billed for things you did not purchase, you can check your credit history to see if a mistake has been made.

- Know how much you owe and how much interest you are paying.

- Borrow money with care and always have a plan for paying back the money that you owe. Don't push off repaying your loan.

Managing Your Credit Cards

Wow! Just sign your name and you can buy whatever you want! Credit cards are fun, handy and... potentially your worst budget crusher. How do you choose the right card? What do you know about your responsibilities as a card holder? Do you know how much interest will accumulate if you can't pay? Keep your finances in good order by learning more about your credit cards.

The Basics:

- Because there are many types of cards out there, you can shop around to find the card that is right for you. What are the interest rates and minimum monthly payments? What will your credit limit be? Does the card offer any bonus features, like points toward "rewards", car rental insurance or affiliation with a cause that you support?

- Know your card. Understand the interest rate, any annual fees, and minimum monthly payments. Make sure you understand all of the terms and conditions <u>before</u> you sign the agreement.

- Keep track of what you purchase with your credit card and where. Then, check your monthly billing statements to ensure that all the charges on it are for purchases that you made. This will help you monitor your spending and avoid fraud.

- Make your minimum payments on time to avoid credit problems. If possible, pay the full balance on your credit card when you receive your bill.

- Only use your credit card if you are sure that you will be able to repay the balance soon. When used wisely, your credit card will help you build a good credit history, which will help you when you apply for a mortgage or a personal loan. When you don't make payments on time, you will hurt your future access to credit.

- If you lose your card or suspect that someone else is using it for unauthorized purchases, call your credit card company immediately. Cancel any credit cards that you are not using.

Credit History and Your Score

Your credit history is recorded by at least one of the U.S.'s three major credit-reporting agencies. A credit report is a "snapshot" of your credit history (i.e. what you borrowed, what you have paid back, late payments, etc.). It is one of the main tools that lenders use to decide whether or not to give you credit. Your credit file is created when you first borrow money or apply for credit. On a regular basis, companies that lend money or issue credit cards to you — including banks, finance companies, credit unions, retailers — send specific factual information related to the financial transactions they have with you to credit reporting agencies.

Your credit score is a judgment about your financial health, at a specific point in time. It indicates the risk you represent for lenders, compared with other consumers.

Some credit-reporting agencies report the lenders' rating of each of your credit history items on a scale of 1 to 9. A rating of "1" means you pay your bills within 30 days of the due date. A rating of "9" means that you never pay your bills. When you apply for credit (whether it is a credit card, loan or mortgage), the loaner will have access to these scores and will use them to assess whether to provide you the credit you are requesting so it is important to keep your score as strong as possible.

Example of a credit report:

AUDREY O'DELL
Consumer Credit Profile
Source: TransUnion

March 12, 2003
This report is available until Apr 11, 2003

Personal Information

Name:	Audrey O'Dell	Current Address:	123 A ST
Also Known As:	Audrey T. O'Dell		HAMILTON, ON L8N 3L2
		Date Updated:	07/2000
Date of Birth:	04/30/1973		
Telephone #:	(123) 456-7890	Previous Address:	456 B ST
			CHARLOTTETOWN, PE C1A 2S8
Employer:	TransUnion	Date Updated:	01/1994
Date Updated:	09/1999		

Consumer Statement

None reported

Summary

Total Accounts:	5	Balances:	4430
Open Accounts:	0	Payments:	110
Closed Accounts:	5	Public Records:	0

Personal information includes your name, aliases, date of birth, phone number, employer, address, and previous addresses.

The **consumer statement** shows any comments you may have made. If, for example, you want to give your side of the story for a disputed delinquency, it appears here.

The **summary section** gives a count of open and closed accounts, delinquencies, estimated total payments and a count of how many credit grantors have looked at your credit report over the last two years.

The main part of your credit file is the **account history**.

For each financial institution that has given you credit, the current account status is shown, as well as a payment history, and summary information.

Your credit report shows how many times you've been 30 days, 60 days, and 90 days late, how much is currently past due, and your credit limit.

You can see when each account was opened, when the creditor most recently reported your status to the credit bureau and whether or not this is a joint account (with responsibility for repayment shared by someone else.)

Summary

Total Accounts:	5	Balances:	4430
Open Accounts:	0	Payments:	110
Closed Accounts:	5	Public Records:	0
Delinquent:	0	Inquiries (2 years):	3
Derogatory:	0		

Account History

At-a-glance viewing of your payment history

		OK		30	90	120	150	PP	RF	CO
Not Open	Unknown	Current	30 days late	60 days late	90 days late	120 days late	150+ days late	Payment plan	Reposession Foreclosure	Collection Chargeoff

Revolving Accounts: Accounts with an open-end term

ZELLERS

Account #:	1245****	Type:	Revolving account	Opened:	04/2002	
Condition:	Open	Pay status:	Paid as Agreed	Reported:	06/09/2004	
Balance:	$345			Responsibility:	Individual account	
High Balance:		Payment:	$10 Monthly (due every month)			
Terms:		Limit:	$1500	Past Due:		

Remarks:

Two Year Payment History:
TransUnion [OK][OK][OK][OK][OK][OK][OK][OK][OK][OK][OK][OK][OK][OK][OK][OK][OK][OK][OK][OK][OK][OK][OK][OK]
jun jul aug sep oct nov dec '03 feb mar apr may jun jul aug sep oct nov dec '04 feb mar apr may

Six Year Payment History:
30 Days Late: 0	60 Days Late: 0	90 Days Late: 0

TD/GM VISA

Account #:		Type:	Revolving account	Opened:	11/2001	
Condition:	Open	Pay status:	Paid as Agreed	Reported:	06/09/2004	
Balance:	$1210			Responsibility:	Individual account	
High Balance:	$1500	Payment:	$0 Monthly (due every month)			
Terms:		Limit:		Past Due:		

Remarks:

Two Year Payment History:
TransUnion [OK][OK][OK][OK][OK][OK][OK][OK][OK][OK][OK][OK][OK][OK][OK][OK][OK][OK][OK][OK][OK][OK][OK][OK]
jun jul aug sep oct nov dec '03 feb mar apr may jun jul aug sep oct nov dec '04 feb mar apr may

Six Year Payment History:
30 Days Late: 0	60 Days Late: 0	90 Days Late: 0

Bank Information

Bank accounts closed for derogatory reasons

None reported

Public Information

None reported

Inquiries

Creditor Name	Date of Inquiry
CDN IMPERIAL BANK OF COM	03/20/2004
CITIBANK CANADA	12/04/2003
TCRS/COTTER	03/08/2003

Creditor Contacts

Creditor Name	Phone Number
None reported	

The Inquiries section displays the creditors that have seen your credit report over the past two years.

Note: While unexpected inquiries or previous addresses can be simple errors, they can be evidence of possible identity theft. Be sure to investigate anything that appears to be incorrect on your credit profile.

Improving your credit score

If your credit score is not as high as you think it should be, make sure that the information in your credit report is correct. To get a copy, go to this website for instructions: AnnualCreditReport.com. To get your credit score only, you may need to pay a small fee.

If it is correct, read your report carefully to find out which factors are having a negative influence on your score, and then work to improve them.

Here are some tips on how to improve your credit score:

1. Always pay your bills on time. Although the payment of your utility bills, such as phone, cable and electricity is not recorded in your credit report, some cell phone companies may report late payments to the credit-reporting agencies which could affect your score.

2. Try to pay your bills in full by the due date. If you aren't able to do this, pay at least the required minimum amount shown on your monthly credit card statement.

3. Try to pay your debts as quickly as possible.

4. Don't go over the credit limit on your credit card. Try to keep your balance well below the limit. The higher your balance, the more impact it has on your credit score.

5. Reduce the number of credit applications you make. If too many potential lenders ask about your credit in a short period of time, this may have a negative effect on your score. However, your score does not change when you ask for information about your own credit report.

6. Make sure you have a credit history. You may have a low score because you do not have a record of owing money and paying it back. You can build a credit history by using a credit card. See the next section to find out how.

Beware of companies that promise to help you re-establish your credit for a fee; their ability to change the information that appears in your credit file is no different than anyone else's! Only your creditors are able to alter this information. Therefore you do not need to pay a third party to obtain, discuss, review or make changes to your credit report.

Beware of any organization that offers to create a new identity and credit file for you. The Federal Trade Commission (FTC) and state attorneys general have filed actions against those who pursue these fraudulent practices. Here are some warning signs that the FTC and others say consumers should look out for to determine if they might be dealing with a credit clinic:

- An organization that guarantees to remove late payments, bankruptcies, or similar information from a credit report

- An organization that charges a lot of money to repair credit

- A company that asks the consumer to write to the credit reporting company and repeatedly seek verification of the same credit account information in the file, month after month, even though the information has been determined to be correct

- An organization that is reluctant to give out their address or one that pushes you to make a decision immediately

How to Beat that Debt

Debt is one of the biggest sources of stress and depression that people experience. That is why it is critical that you learn to conquer your debt issues. Three basic ways are:

- Plan your spending according to your income

- Don't get into more debt

- Manage your existing debt

Have you lost control of your finances? How can you beat that debt? Here are ten things you can do to help your situation.

Plan your spending according to your income.

a. Keep track of spending and make a budget.

One of the smartest things you can do to get control of your finances is to start keeping track of what you spend so that you can see exactly where your money is going each month. This is the first step in creating a budget that shows your income and expenses.

Having a budget and learning to stick to it will help you free up money to reduce your debt. For more information on budgeting, see the "Budget Worksheet" later in this module.

b. Put needs before wants.

Buy what you need first. Eliminate unnecessary expenses and look for things you can live without. See the "Needs vs. Wants" section later in this module.

Don't get into more debt.

a. Keep your credit card in your wallet.

To avoid getting into more debt, use cash or your debit card instead of your credit card. That way, you'll be spending money you already have.

b. Avoid 'Buy Now, Pay Later' promotions.

When you're having problems making ends meet, the administrative fees tied to such offers and high interest rates if you don't pay on time will only add to your existing debt load.

c. Reduce small, recurring expenses.

Saving a little every day can go a long way. Good examples of ways you can save on costs include taking public transit instead of your car, bringing your lunch to work and reducing your coffee consumption. Eliminating that extra $2.50 coffee or $4.00 latte each workday can mean over $600 - $1,000 a year in savings.

d. Reduce your banking fees.

Use automated teller machines (ATMs) from your own financial institution. When you use your debit card in the ATM of another bank, you will be charged by *both* banks an extra fee of $1.50 each. Review your banking package every now and then to make sure that it is still the best one for you.

Manage your existing debt.

a. Pay down your highest interest rate debts first.

If you carry a balance on your credit card, then this is likely the debt with the highest interest rate. Use cash or a debit card while you pay off this debt to avoid accumulating more.

While you pay off the credit card debt, don't forget to make the minimum payments on other debts with lower interest rates. If you set aside the main part of your income towards bringing the balance down on your most expensive loan, you'll be surprised at how much you save.

b. **Contact your creditors.**

As soon as you realize that you are having trouble making ends meet, call your creditors and explain the situation. In most cases, they will work out a modified payment plan that will make it easier for you to pay off your debt.

c. **Get a consolidation loan with your financial institution.**

This means getting one single loan to pay off all your existing debts so that you have just one payment to make. For this new loan to save you money it must have a lower interest rate and a lower monthly payment than all the other loans put together. It is also important to stop using any credit cards that you consolidated into the new loan. For more information on a consolidation loan, talk to your bank or financial professional.

d. **Talk to trusted financial professionals.**

These may include your bank representative, your financial planner or a credit counselling agency. With their help, you will be able to evaluate your current debt situation, determine your present and future needs, make a budget and find ways to pay off the debt.

"Debt is like any other trap, easy enough to get into,
hard enough to get out of."
– Henry Wheeler Shaw

Fraud: Watch Out!

There are numerous scams and frauds out there so you really need to be alert to the bills that come in.

Credit card charges

Check your credit card statement very closely each month to verify that those charges are all yours. Sometimes people will either deliberately or accidentally charge your card for purchases that you didn't make or a charge may be doubled in error. If this is the case, contact the credit card company immediately and file a claim to get it removed.

Collection Agency Scams

If you owe debt, the company that you owe the debt to may hire a collection agency to collect the debt from you. If you do owe this money, then you need to pay it to resolve the issue before it ends up in court. However, there are times when collection agencies may call you or send you a notice about a debt that is not yours. If this is the case, you do not need to pay it which is why you should be very careful about being pressured into paying something that you don't owe. If this is the case, you need to respond to the notice via registered mail even if you dispute it. Review your rights on the Industry Canada site under Office of Consumer Affairs.

Other scams to be aware of:

Faked E-Commerce Websites

It begins when you receive an email that lures you to what you think is a legitimate website run by a real company (though it's not). Then you're tricked into divulging your personal information (credit card info, etc.). Banks will never email you if there is a problem with your account.

Pharming

This scam occurs when a hacker manages to redirect a website's traffic to another bogus website.

Auction Fraud

Online auction fraud involves the misrepresentation of an advertised product through an Internet auction site, the non-delivery of an item purchased through an Internet auction site (e.g. eBay) or a non-payment for goods purchased through an Internet auction site.

Job Offering Scams

Here is the setup: a company is looking for people who can receive payments from the company's "customers". They will then have to wire those funds to the company by Western Union, minus a fee they receive for every payment forwarded. The position is often described as a "Correspondence Manager", "Transfer Manager", "Financial Agent" or "Shipping Manager". This type of scam involves criminal activity (i.e. money laundering) and the job seeker is needed to break the money trail so police can't investigate the real criminal. Unfortunately, the job seeker can be charged with money laundering by police.

Social Networking sites

Scammers browse social network sites (e.g. MySpace, Facebook, etc.) for personal details that have been posted by users in order to commit identity theft.

Advance Fee loans

Ads promising "money to loan . . . regardless of credit history" lure you into paying fees that range from $25 to several hundred dollars in advance of supposedly receiving loans that are "guaranteed". Often, these ads feature "900" numbers, which result in charges on your phone bill, or toll-free out-of-state or country "800" numbers. The fee may be called "processing", "application" or "first month's payment". In most instances, you will not receive the promised loan, never hearing from the loan company again, or will be told later that you are ineligible for the credit.

Phishing

This is the attempt to steal sensitive information such as usernames, passwords and credit card details by pretending to be a trustworthy online contact. Emails or IMs claiming to be from popular social web sites, auction sites, online payment processors or IT Administrators are commonly used to lure unsuspecting victims. Phishing often tricks users to enter details at a fake website whose look and feel are almost identical to the legitimate one.

Vishing

This is a telephone version of Phishing. When the victim answers the call, an automated recording is played to alert the victim that his/her credit card has had fraudulent activity or that their bank account has had unusual activity. The message instructs the victim to call the following phone number immediately. The same phone number is often shown in the spoofed caller ID and given the same name as the financial company they are pretending to represent. When the victim calls the number, it is answered by automated instructions to enter their credit card number or bank account number on the key pad. Once the victim enters their credit card number or bank account number, the "visher" has the information necessary to make fraudulent use of the card or to access the account. The call is often used to collect additional details such as security PIN, expiration date, date of birth, etc.

SMishing

Similar to phishing, smishing uses cell phone text messages to deliver the "bait" to get you to reveal your personal information. The "hook" in the text message may be a web site URL; however it has become more common to see a phone number that connects to automated voice response system. This is an example of a smishing message in current circulation:

"Notice - this is an automated message from (a local credit union), your ATM card has been suspended. To reactivate, call urgent at 866-###-####."

In many cases, the smishing message will show that it came from "5000" instead of displaying an actual phone number. This usually indicates the SMS message was sent via email to the cell phone, and not sent from another cell phone. This information is then used to credit duplicate credit/debit/ATM cards. There are actual cases where information entered on a fraudulent web site was used to create a credit or debit card that was used halfway around the world, within 30 minutes.

False Charities

Bogus charities often use names that are very close to the names of legitimate and respected charities. The end of the year is the peak season for charity appeals. It also is the peak season for the bogus charity appeals.

Warning signs:

- High pressure or threatening telemarketers who want you to contribute immediately.

- Someone calls and thanks you for a pledge you don't remember making.

- Copycat names. Names that might be misleading or deceiving.

Dating Services

A typical Internet dating scam goes like this:

1.   A person registers at an online dating service and creates a profile. The profile will include information and possibly a photograph, along with contact details.

2.   A scammer contacts the person posing as someone interested in a romantic relationship.

3.   The victim responds and the pair begins corresponding regularly. They may soon bypass the dating service contact system and start communicating directly, usually via email.

4.   The scammer will slowly earn the trust of the victim. S/he may discuss family, jobs and other details designed to make the scammer seem like a real person who is genuinely interested in the victim. Photographs may be exchanged. However, the "person" that the victim thinks s/he is corresponding with is likely to be purely an invention of the scammer. Photographs sent by the scammer are not real. The victim's "love interest" may not even be the same gender that s/he claims to be.

5.   After the scammer has established the illusion of a genuine and meaningful relationship, s/he will begin asking the victim for money. For example, the scammer may claim that he or she wants to meet in-person and ask the victim to send money for an airfare so that a meeting can take place. Or the scammer may claim that there has been a family medical emergency and request financial assistance. The scammer may use a variety of excuses to entice the victim to send funds.

6.   If the victim complies and sends money, s/he will probably receive further such requests. With his or her judgement clouded by a growing love for the scammer's imaginary character, s/he may continue to send money.

7.   Finally, the victim will come to realize that s/he has been duped, perhaps after waiting fruitlessly at the airport for a "lover" who, will, of course, never arrive.

8.   Meanwhile, the scammer pockets the money and moves on to the next victim. In fact, the scammer may be stringing along several victims simultaneously.

In many cases, the victim will not only have lost out financially, but will also be left feeling broken-hearted. These scammers tend to prey on victims that may be especially lonely, shy or isolated and therefore more vulnerable.

Public Access Computers

Public access computers include computers shared by strangers (e.g. libraries, schools, internet cafés, etc.). Do not use these for logging into online bank accounts or any other confidential sites. It is possible that scammers have installed applications, such as Keylogger, that secretly record keyboard key strokes, therefore, easily accessing your passwords. And if you forget to log out, people can access your account.

Malware/Intrusion

This involves software designed to infiltrate or damage a computer system. Malware includes computer viruses, worms, trojan horses, spyware, dishonest adware, crimeware and other malicious and unwanted software.

Telephone lottery scams

'Winners' are congratulated on the big prize but before they can claim they must send money to pay for taxes and processing fees. Many of these scams deceptively use the name of a real lottery.

Investment related scams

An unsolicited phone call will invite you to invest in shares, fine wine, gemstones etc. These "investments" are usually very high risk, not listed on any stock exchange and will be difficult to sell if you do purchase them.

Nigerian advance fee or "419" frauds

This scam takes the form of an offer asking you to share in a huge amount of money in return for using your bank account to allow the transfer of the money out of the country. The scammers will either use the information given to empty your bank account or they will convince you that your money is needed up front for bribing officials.

Pyramid schemes

These schemes offer a financial investment based upon the number of new recruits to the scheme. Investors are misled about the likely returns as there are not enough people to support the scheme indefinitely – only the organizers make enough.

Matrix schemes

These are promoted via website offering pricey techie gadgets as free gifts in return for spending $20 or similar on a low-cost product such as a mobile telephone booster. Consumers who buy the product then join a waiting list to receive their free gift. The person at the top of the list gets their free gift only after a prescribed number – sometimes as high as 100 – of new members join up. In reality, most of those on the list never get their expensive gift.

Credit scams

Advertisements appear in local papers offering fast loans regardless of credit history. Consumers who respond are told their loans have been approved but before the money can be released they must pay a fee to cover insurance. Once the advance fee is paid, the company and the loan disappear.

Property investment schemes

Would-be property millionaires attend a free presentation before being persuaded to hand over thousands of dollars for a property course encouraging them to invest in properties. The properties involved are usually derelict or non-existent.

Work at home and business opportunity schemes

This scam works by advertising for "paid work from home" opportunities which nearly always demand up front money for materials or by requiring investment in a business with little or no chance of success.

Health Care Fraud or Health Insurance Fraud

There are various types of health care-related frauds.

Medical Equipment Fraud: Equipment manufacturers offer "free" products to individuals. Insurers are then charged for products that were not needed and/or may not have been delivered.

"Rolling Lab" Schemes: Unnecessary and sometimes fake tests are given to individuals at health clubs, retirement homes, or shopping malls and billed to insurance companies or Medicare.

Services Not Performed: Customers or providers bill insurers for services never rendered by changing bills or submitting fake ones.

Medicare Fraud: Medicare fraud can take the form of any of the health insurance frauds described above. Senior citizens are frequent targets of Medicare schemes, especially by medical equipment manufacturers who offer seniors free medical products in exchange for their Medicare numbers. Because a physician has to sign a form certifying that equipment or testing is needed before Medicare pays for it, con artists fake signatures or bribe corrupt doctors to sign the forms. Once a signature is in place, the manufacturers bill Medicare for merchandise or service that was not needed or was not ordered.

Debt Collection Fraud

You get a notice or a call from a collection agency stating that you owe money on a credit purchase that you never made. They will harass you at home, work and on your cell if they find out those numbers. If you did not make this charge, demand in writing to see the original receipt signed by you. If they cannot produce that, then they have no claim.

"Ponzi' Schemes

"Ponzi" schemes promise high financial returns or dividends not available through traditional investments. Instead of investing the funds of victims, however, the con artist pays "dividends" to initial investors using the funds of subsequent investors. The scheme generally falls apart when the operator flees with all of the proceeds or when a sufficient number of new investors cannot be found to allow the continued payment of "dividends."

Gift Card Scam

Be careful when purchasing gift cards through auction sites or classified ads. It is safest to purchase gift cards directly from the merchant or retail store. If the gift card merchant discovers that your card is fraudulent, the merchant will deactivate the gift card and refuse to honor it for purchases. Victims of this scam lose the money paid for the gift card purchase.

Claims of Being Stranded Scams

Portraying to be the victim, the hacker uses the victim's account to send a notice to their contacts. The notice claims the victim is in immediate need of money due to being robbed of their credit cards, passport, money, and cell phone; leaving them stranded in Europe or some other location or being arrested out-of-town. Some claim they only have a few days to pay their hotel bill and promise to reimburse upon their return home. A sense of urgency to help their friend/contact may cause the recipient to fail to validate the claim, increasing the likelihood of them falling for this scam.

If you receive a similar notice and are not sure it is a scam, you should always verify the information before sending any money.

Mystery/Secret Shopper Scams

Many retail and service corporations hire evaluators to perform secret or random checks on themselves or their competitors, and fraudsters are capitalizing on this employment opportunity.

Victims were contacted via e-mail and U.S. mail to apply to be a mystery shopper. Applicants are asked to send a resume and are purportedly subject to an extensive background check before being accepted as a mystery shopper. The employees are sent a check with instructions to shop at a specified retailer for a specific length of time and spend a specific amount on merchandise from the store. The employees receive instructions to take note of the store's environment, color, payment procedures, gift items, and shopping/carrier bags and report back to the employer. The second evaluation is the ease and accuracy of wiring money from the retail location. The money to be wired is also included in the check sent to the employee. The remaining balance is the employee's payment for the completion of the assignment. After merchandise is purchased and money is wired, the employees are advised by the bank the check cashed was counterfeit, and they are responsible for the money lost in addition to bank fees incurred.

In other versions of the scheme, applicants are requested to provide bank account information to have money directly deposited into their accounts. The fraudster then has acquired access to these victims' accounts and can withdraw money, which makes the applicant a victim of identity theft.

Identity Theft

Identity theft is a crime in which an imposter obtains key pieces of your personal information, such as your banking information or your driver's license number, in order to impersonate you. The information can be used to obtain credit, merchandise, and services in your name or to provide the thief with false credentials. In addition to running up debt, an imposter might provide false identification to police, creating a criminal record or leaving outstanding arrest warrants in your name. There are two basic versions of financial identity theft

1. **Victim Established Accounts Accessed**

    The scammer pretends to be an existing account holder in order to obtain funds from the legitimate bank account of the victim. This involves obtaining one or more identity tokens (Social Security card, paper check, deposit slip, PIN code, debit/credit card number, bank statement, identifying personal data, etc.) then using the ID token to access funds via one or more methods (branch teller, ATM, retail cashier, telephone banking, etc.).

2. **Scammer Established Accounts**

    The scammer establishes new accounts using someone else's identity or a fake identity. Typically the intent is to use someone else's good credit history to obtain funds (credit cards or loans) or a checking account which can be overdrafted (i.e. allowed withdraw more money than is in the account). A classic example of credit-dependent financial crime (bank fraud) occurs when a scammer obtains a loan from a financial institution by impersonating someone else. The scammer pretends to be the victim by presenting an accurate name, address, birth date, or other information that the lender requires as a way of establishing identity. Even if this information is checked against the data at a national consumer reporting agency, the bank will encounter no concerns, as all of the victim's information matches the records. The bank has no easy way to discover that the person is pretending to be the victim, especially if an original, government-issued id can't be verified (as is the case in online, mail, telephone, and fax-based transactions). The scammer keeps the money from the loan, the bank is never repaid, and the victim is wrongly blamed for defaulting on a loan s/he never authorized.

In most cases, a scammer needs to obtain personal id or documents about an individual in order to impersonate them. Some ways that they may do this by:

- Stealing mail or rummaging through garbage.

- Retrieving information from old equipment, like computers, that have been disposed of carelessly, e.g. at public dump sites, given away without proper sanitizing etc.

- Stealing payment or identification cards, either by pick pocketing or by skimming through a compromised card reader.

- Eavesdropping on public transactions to obtain personal data (shoulder surfing).

- Stealing personal information from computers and computer databases (Trojan horses, hacking and Keylogger keystroke recording software).

- Data breach that results in the public (i.e. posted on the internet) or easily-obtainable (i.e. printed on a mailing label) display of sensitive information such as a Social Insurance Number or credit card number.

- Advertising bogus job offers (either full-time or work from home based) to which the victims will reply with their full name, address, resume, telephone numbers, and banking details.

- Infiltration of organizations that store large amounts of personal information.

- Impersonating a trusted company/institution/organization in an electronic communication to promote revealing of personal information (phishing).

- Browsing social network (MySpace, Facebook, etc) sites, online for personal details that have been posted by users.

Tips for Avoiding Fraud

(Courtesy usa.gov)

- Don't buy from an unfamiliar company. Legitimate businesses understand that you want more information about their company and are happy to comply.

- Always ask for and wait until you receive written material about any offer or charity. If you get brochures about costly investments, ask someone whose financial advice you trust to review them. But, unfortunately, beware—not everything written down is true.

- Always check out unfamiliar companies with your local consumer protection agency, Better Business Bureau, state attorney general, the National Fraud Information Center, or other watchdog groups. Unfortunately, not all bad businesses can be identified through these organizations.

- Obtain a salesperson's name, business identity, telephone number, street address, mailing address, and business license number before you conduct business. Some con artists give out false names, telephone numbers, addresses, and business license numbers. Verify the accuracy of these items.

- Before you give money to a charity or make an investment, find out what percentage of the money is paid in commissions and what percentage actually goes to the charity or investment.

- Before you send money, ask yourself a simple question. "What guarantee do I really have that this salesperson will use my money in the manner we agreed upon?"

- Don't pay in advance for services. Pay services only after they are delivered.

- Be wary of companies that want to send a messenger to your home to pick up money, claiming it is part of their service to you. In reality, they are taking your money without leaving any trace of whom they are or where they can be reached.

- Always take your time making a decision. Legitimate companies won't pressure you to make a snap decision.

- Don't pay for a "free prize." If a caller tells you the payment is for taxes, he or she is violating federal law.

- Before you receive your next sales pitch, decide what your limits are—the kinds of financial information you will and won't give out on the telephone.

- Be sure to talk over big investments offered by telephone salespeople with a trusted friend, family member, or financial advisor. It's never rude to wait and think about an offer.

- Never respond to an offer you don't understand thoroughly.

- Never send money or give out personal information such as credit card numbers and expiration dates, bank account numbers, dates of birth, or social security numbers to unfamiliar companies or unknown persons.

- Be aware that your personal information is often brokered to telemarketers through third parties.

- If you have been victimized once, be wary of persons who call offering to help you recover your losses for a fee paid in advance.

- If you have information about a fraud, report it to state, local, or federal law enforcement agencies.

- Don't give out your credit card number online unless the site is a secure and reputable. Sometimes a tiny icon of a padlock appears to symbolize a higher level of security to transmit data. This icon is not a guarantee of a secure site, but provides some assurance.

- Don't trust a site just because it claims to be secure.

- Before using the site, check out the security/encryption software it uses.

- Do your homework on the individual or company to ensure that they are legitimate.

- Obtain a physical address rather than simply a post office box and a telephone number, and call the seller to see if the telephone number is correct and working.

- Send an e-mail to the seller to make sure the e-mail address is active, and be wary of those that utilize free e-mail services where a credit card wasn't required to open the account.

- Consider not purchasing from sellers who won't provide you with this type of information.

- Check with the Better Business Bureau from the seller's area.

- Check out other websites regarding this person/company.

- Don't judge a person or company by their website. Flashy websites can be set up quickly.

- Be cautious when responding to special investment offers, especially through unsolicited e-mail.

- Be cautious when dealing with individuals/companies from outside your own country.

- If possible, purchase items online using your credit card, because you can often dispute the charges if something goes wrong.

- Make sure the transaction is secure when you electronically send your credit card number.

- Keep a list of all your credit cards and account information along with the card issuer's contact information. If anything looks suspicious or you lose your credit card(s), contact the card issuer immediately.

- Do not believe the promise of large sums of money for your cooperation.

- Guard your account information carefully.

Budgets: Making a Plan

Learn to Manage Your Money

Remember when your biggest expense was candy and comic books? Well, for most of us, that has changed! As an adult, you are responsible for managing your own finances. Here are a few things you should know.

- First, do you have financial goals? Do you have a plan for how you will reach them? Can you afford to take time to get informed about financial planning, smart consumer decision-making and debt management? Can you afford not to?

- Use a notebook to list all of your income and expenses for one month to gain better understanding of your spending habits. From your morning coffee to a new home theatre system, you need to know where your money is going.

- Establish a budget and stick to it! This will help indicate if you are spending more than you should. Do you need to make some changes? Careful financial planning will help you save money for a car, a new laptop, a new video game or whatever else suits your needs!

- Watch your debt! Know how much you owe and how much the interest is costing you. Some debt may be necessary to pay for school, a car or a house. Try to avoid going into debt to pay for non-essential items such as an 3DTV, video games, clothes, and so on. The interest could get expensive!

- Start saving! If you can, put away some money every month, even if it's just a few dollars. The money will start to add-up over time and be there when you need it.

- It's all about making choices: what can you do without *now* so that you can have something else *later?* In the end, you'll enjoy your life more knowing that you will still have money to save or spend after all of your bills are paid. Moderation is the key!

Making a Budget and Sticking to It

Do you shiver whenever you hear the word "budget"? Sure, a budget involves a bit of work on your part, but the payoff is financial stability and peace of mind. Once you get the hang of it, budgeting is easy and can mean a better financial future for yourself.

What is a budget?

A budget is a written document (not a mental list) that helps you take control of your personal finances. It is an excellent money management tool that can help you in any of the following situations:

- If you find that money is tight.

- If you don't know where your money is going.

- If you have problems paying off your debt.

- If you don't save regularly.

- If you want to find ways to make your dollar stretch further.

A budget helps you see more clearly how much money you receive and how much you spend and save. It helps you set spending limits and live within your means. It helps you find ways to get rid of your debt, reduce costs and have more money for things that are *really* important to you.

Before you start making a budget

Think about your goals

Before you start making a budget, take some time to think about your financial goals. Do you want to pay off your debt? Do you want to go on vacation or buy a specific item for yourself or someone else? Do you want to go to college or university? Do you want a car or your own place? Do you want to spend a year travelling?

Keep track of your money

Most people know how much money they make (income). But do you know where your money is going (expenses)? The following exercise will help you achieve just that. Every dollar you spend has an impact on the overall picture.

✍ Exercise: Tracking Your Habits

Every day, for a month or two, keep track of everything you buy, from groceries to your daily cup of coffee. Keep a copy of bills you pay during that time, and write down what you buy in a notepad or keep your receipts. Doing this will help you understand your spending habits and make a budget.

Needs vs. Wants

How often do the words "I need" come out of your mouth? "I need that coat!", "I need that iPod in green even though I already have one in blue and one in pink!", "I need that mochaccino!". But did you ever stop to think how many of those requests are actually *"needs"* and how many are simply *"wants"*?

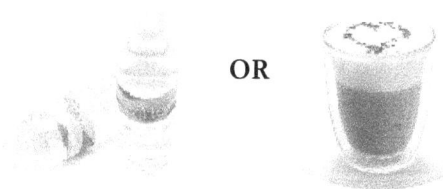

To live on a budget, it helps to really understand the difference between *"needs"* and *"wants"*. And you probably do understand that food is a need and a latte is a want. But some mornings, after taking care of your baby brother or working late, a latte is sure to feel like a *"need"*. Maybe coffee is a *"need"* but gourmet coffee drinks are definitely a *"want"*. Maybe a cell phone is a *"need"* for personal safety but custom ringtones are almost assuredly a *"want"*. When creating a spending plan and trying to live with limited funds, it's helpful to really consider what is a *"need"* and what is a *"want"*.

What you define as needs and wants does not have to remain etched in stone. For example, having the newest iPad could generally be defined as a want. But if you find that noise from your siblings or the neighbours is too distracting for you to study, you might need background music to block out the other sounds.

✒ Exercise: Needs vs. Wants Worksheet

Use the Needs vs. Wants Worksheet to write down some of your *"needs"* and *"wants"*. Then look carefully at what you've written down. Are the *"needs"* really *"needs"*, or can they be moved to the *"wants"* category?

Now, review your list and think about what's really important to you and what has lasting value. Be realistic (and honest)!

- Do you really need or want everything on your list? Put stars next to the items that are particularly important to you.

- Are some needs really wants? Cross off the least important wants.

- Decide if each item makes sense. If not, cross it off, or change it to something that is more reasonable.

Did this help you identify ways to save money and meet your goals?

Needs Vs. Wants Worksheet

Use this worksheet to write down some of your needs and wants and then look carefully at what you've written down.

Review your list and think about what's really important to you and why.

- Do you really need or want *everything* on your list? Put checkmarks next to the items that are particularly important to you.

- Can some needs really be wants in disguise? Cross off the least important wants.

- If you find that some of your wants are unreasonable, write down a more reasonable alternative to that particular want.

For example: is a cell phone a need or a want? Some say it is a want as you don't *need* a cell phone to survive (it is not food or shelter). However, some feel that it is a need for security and contact. So you may list it as a need but list it as a pre-paid plan instead of a monthly plan as the former is usually quite cheaper.

Needs	Cost	Wants	Cost	Alternatives to Wants

Budget Worksheet

Budgeting is one of the biggest challenges for most people. It is a great reality check if you take it seriously and are honest with your needs and wants that you listed above. For example, if money is tight then maybe you don't need all those additional features on your phone like conferencing and call waiting which can add up. Maybe you don't need the VIP package listed on your cable bill if you don't watch all those TV channels.

Making a budget involves comparing the amount of money you think you will receive (your income), spend (your expenses) and save with the amount of money that you actually receive, spend and save over a fixed period of time. Your budget is balanced when your income equals or is greater than your expenses.

And please be honest when making your budget. Don't assume if your cell phone bill was $150 last month that you will always pare it down to $50 per month. If some of your bills vary month to month, average them over the past 12 bills.

As you fill out the *Budget Worksheet*, follow the steps below to create a balanced budget and find ways to reach your financial goals.

How to use the Budget Worksheet

Step	How to use the Budget Worksheet
Step 1: **List your previous incomes and expenses**	• Take out the recent pay stubs, bills and receipts you collected over the previous month(s). Try not to go by memory. • Separate your income and expenses in the categories listed. For each category, if you have collected data for more than one month, take the average. Add any missing categories under 'Other'. **When you are done, review the figures and ask yourself:** • Did I miss any income or expenses? • In the 'Mandatory Expenses (Needs)' and 'Other Expenses (Wants)' sections, are there any other categories missing to reflect my personal situation? • Are there categories in the 'Mandatory Expenses (Needs)' that fit better in the 'Other Expenses (Wants)', or vice-versa, to reflect my personal situation? • Was I able to save any money, or did I have to borrow (such as adding money to a credit card balance) to make ends meet?
Step 2: **Create a balanced budget**	Creating a budget means looking at your past expenses and creating an improved version that reflects your financial goals. A balanced budget is when income exceeds expenses—that is, you are able to save a bit of money each month. This is the ideal scenario. Your budget is what will guide your spending in future months and help you save money. • Take another copy of the worksheet and complete it using your ideal situation. Use the results from Step 1 to guide you, but adjust the figures as you go along, while you think of the following:

	• Do the figures in the first worksheet reflect my expenses in *any* given month? If not, what would be a more realistic figure? • Are there any small, recurring expenses that I can cut? • Are there expenses in the "Wants" categories that I can cut? • Do I want to add money to certain new spending categories that reflect my financial goals, such as saving for a vacation or school or creating an emergency fund? Once you are done, take total income and deduct total expenses to find out how much money you will be able to save. Adjust your expenses where you can so that your monthly savings help you meet your future goals.

Step 3:
Use your
budget each
month
	This is the most important step in the budget process. Each month, limit your spending as much as possible to what was in your second worksheet. Keep receipts, bills and lists of your income and expenses.
	
	FILL OUT ANOTHER WORKSHEET TO TRACK HOW YOU ARE DOING (Actual Spending) at the end of each month (you may want to make extra copies of the *Budget Worksheet* for this purpose) using the data you collected during the month.
	
	COMPARE WORKSHEET #2 AND WORKSHEET #3 (Difference between Actual Spending and Budget)
	
	• To help you figure out whether your spending for the month was in line with your budget, you can fill out another worksheet to track your progress.
	
	• Look at the results of worksheet #4 and ask yourself the following questions:
	
	    • Are the differences between my actual spending and my budget large or small?
	
	    • In which categories are the differences the largest? Why? Is it because of an unusual situation or is this likely to happen each month?
	
	    • Am I able to save enough money to reach my financial goals or to pay off my debt?
	
	Continue with this exercise each month. Many people make this a regular habit at the end of each month.

Budget Worksheet

INCOME ITEMS

Net Income Or Self-Employment Earnings (After Taxes)	
Income From Investments/Interest	
Government Grants/Subsidies (After Taxes)	
Allowance	
Unemployment Insurance/ Worker's Comp. Earnings	
Other Earnings -	
- Public Assistance	
- Lawsuit settlements/Lottery winnings/Annuities	
Total Monthly Income (A) (add all income items)	

MANDATORY EXPENSE ITEMS (NEEDS)

Rent/Mortgage	
Room & Board	
Property Taxes/Condo Fees (1/12 of annual total)	
Home Insurance	
Utilities (gas, hydro, water) (average is 25% of rent)	
Tuition	
Groceries	
Prescription Drugs	
Child Care	
Doctor	
Dentist	
Nursing Care	
Family Court Payments	
Tax Provisions	
Household repairs	

Basic Clothing	
Loan Payments	
Life, Disability, Medical Insurance	
Mandatory Savings/Emergency Fund	
Other	
Car Expenses:	
Lease/ Loan Payment	
License/Plate Registration	
Repairs/Maintenance	
Gas	
Insurance	

OTHER EXPENSE ITEMS (WANTS)

Telephone
    ■ Home Phone
    ■ Long Distance Plan
    ■ Cell Phone	

Non-essential Clothing	
Laundry/Dry Cleaning	
Toiletries	
Haircuts	
Meals Outside Home (restaurants, etc.)	
Lunches	
Internet	
Cable Television	

Furniture Payments
    ■ Can you live on milk crates? $40/month
    ■ Used couches are fine. $80/month
    ■ I deserve all new! $250/month	

Cigarettes	
Alcohol	
Recreation/Entertainment	

Children's Activities	
Gifts	
Donations	
Transportation (other than auto) Public Transit Pass/month	
Vacations	
Other (specify)	

Total Monthly Expenses (B) (add all expense items)	-

Total Monthly Income (A)	(from above)	-
Total Monthly Expenses (B)	(from above)	-
Excess (Deficiency): (A-B)*		-

*If the number is a negative (i.e. expenses are greater than income) then you are spending more than you are earning.

Learning to stick to your budget

Learning to stick to a budget can seem difficult at first, but the more you use your budget, the easier it becomes.

Evaluate your budget from time-to-time

If you find that your actual spending varies a lot from your budget, you will have to re-adjust the figures in your budget to make it more realistic. In this case, go back to step 2 and reduce certain expenses or restrict your spending in certain categories.

If your actual spending varies only a little from your budget, you are on the right track.

If you are not saving enough or are not able pay off your debt, find other ways to cut down on expenses and adjust your budget accordingly.

Keep up the good work!

If you can stick to your budget quite closely, you should find that your income covers your expenses and that you are saving enough for your financial goals.

Cost of Living

When budgeting, you always need to keep in mind the current cost of necessities. As prices increase far more often than they decrease, you should be aware of some of the typical expenses that you may encounter.

2010 Housing Prices

Take note of the median housing prices for your region compared to other regions in the country. More importantly, take notice of the Qualifying Household Income required to gain a mortgage.

Standard Condo

Region	Price	Qualifying Household Income*
Atlanta	$69,000	$38,539
Baltimore	$225,500	$80,926
Boston	$275,300	$97,047
Chicago	$137,000	$55,660
Dallas	$130,000	$53,818
Detroit	$66,000	$37,784
Houston	$120,000	$51,380
Las Vegas	$50,000	$33,755
Los Angeles	$245,000	$87,238
Miami	$75,000	$40,050
Nashville	$163,500	$62,332
New York City	$635,000	$213,000
Philadelphia	$188,000	$68,786
Phoenix	$70,000	$38,791
San Francisco	$250,000	$88,857
Seattle	$165,000	$62,710

Qualifying income is the minimum annual income used by lenders to measure the ability of a borrower to make mortgage payments. Typically, no more than 32% of a borrower's gross annual income should go to "mortgage expenses" — principal, interest, property taxes and heating costs (plus maintenance fees for condos).

Standard Single Family House

Region	Price	Qualifying Household Income*
Atlanta	$114,000	$$48,869
Baltimore	$285,000	$100,000
Boston	$345,000	$120,000
Chicago	$175,000	$65,228
Dallas	$115,000	$50,121
Detroit	$55,000	$35,014
Houston	$106,000	$47,855
Las Vegas	$120,000	$51,380
Los Angeles	$350,000	$121,000
Miami	$168,000	$63,465
Nashville	$134,000	$54,905
New York City	$334,000	$116,000
Philadelphia	$227,660	$81,622
Phoenix	$118,500	$51,002
San Francisco	$400,000	$137,000
Seattle	$285,000	$100,000

Qualifying income is the minimum annual income used by lenders to measure the ability of a borrower to make mortgage payments. Typically, no more than 32% of a borrower's gross annual income should go to "mortgage expenses" — principal, interest, property taxes and heating costs (plus maintenance fees for condos).

2009 Average Monthly Rent For Two-Bedroom Apartments

Region	Rent
Atlanta	$878
Baltimore	$1,037
Boston	$1,345
Chicago	$1,004
Dallas	$905
Detroit	$809
Houston	$866
Las Vegas	$1,013
Los Angeles	$1,361
Miami	$1,156
Nashville	$761
New York City	$1,313
Philadelphia	$1,005
Phoenix	$877
San Francisco	$1,658
Seattle	$987
National Average	$928

Source: Wtnrradio.com

A household must earn $37,105 a year to afford the national average two-bedroom fair-market rent of $928 a month. A full-time worker would have to make $17.84 an hour to afford the average 2 bedroom if no more than the recommended guideline of 30 percent of income is spent on housing.

2009 Average Annual Expenditure Per Household

Concept	Food	Shelter	Utilities	Transportation	Health Care
USA	$6,372	$10,075	$3,645	$7,658	$3,126
Atlanta	$5,375	$10,639	$3,899	$6,760	$2,417
Baltimore	$5,931	$13,617	$4,209	$6,621	$2,973
Boston	$8,167	$12,857	$4,248	$8,591	$3,453
Chicago	$7,037	$13,116	$4,052	$8,840	$3,485
Cleveland	$5,737	$8,820	$3,837	$7,010	$3,315
Dallas	$6,734	$10,253	$4,275	$8,689	$3,032
Detroit	$6,412	$9,635	$3,791	$9,463	$2,672
Houston	$7,009	$10,776	$4,505	$10,843	$3,267
Los Angeles	$7,531	$14,938	$3,257	$8,784	$2,620
Miami/Ft. Laud	$5,803	$12,592	$3,740	$8,427	$1,565
Minneapolis	$6,887	$11,852	$3,513	$8,833	$3,314
New York	$7,420	$15,482	$4,309	$8,495	$3,027
Philadelphia	$6,460	$13,597	$4,444	$8,202	$3,036
Phoenix	$6,402	$11,185	$3,892	$9,330	$3,326
San Diego	$6,541	$15,146	$2,989	$7,171	$2,249
San Francisco	$7,952	$19,096	$3,139	$9,535	$3,319
Seattle	$8,082	$13,829	$3,554	$9,380	$3,684
Washington	$7,835	$16,842	$3,977	$9,563	$3,239

Source: U.S. Census. 2012.

Public Transportation

City	Regular		Student*	
	Per Ride	**Monthly**	**Per Ride**	**Monthly**
Atlanta	$2.50	$95	$2.50	$68.50
Baltimore	$1.60	$64	$1.60	$39
Boston	$2	$70	$1	$28
Chicago	$2.25	$86	$1	N/A
Dallas	$1.75	$65	$0.85	N/A
Detroit	$2	$66	$1	$33
Las Vegas	$2	$65	$1	$30
Los Angeles	$1.50	$75	$1.50	$24/$36
Miami	$2	$100	$2	$50
Nashville	$1.70	$84	$1	$58.50
New York	$2.25	$104	$2.25	$104
Philadelphia	$2	$83	$2	$83
Phoenix	$1.75	$55	$0.85	$27.50
San Francisco	$2	$64	$0.75	$22
Seattle	$2.25	$81	$1.25	$45

*Different youth/student passes exist so check with the one that is right for your circumstances.

Cost of Car Ownership

Everybody wants to own a car. In some locations, you need a car to get around as there isn't sufficient public transit. But do you really realize the cost of owning a car? Not just the payments, but the gas, maintenance, insurance, plate renewals, etc. And if you really don't need the car, what could that expense have provided for you if you hadn't spent it on the car. Here is an example:

Expense	2011 Mazda 3 $23,588	2003 Ford Mustang $8,840
Annual Purchase Cost (over 5 years)	$4,717	$1,762
Annual Finance Charges (7.5%)	$954	$357
Gas & Motor Oil	$1,730	$2,250
Annual Maintenance & Repairs	$500	$700
Annual Car Insurance	$1,177	$953
Licensing and other fees.	$100	$100
Monthly Costs	**$764.83**	**$549.91**
If you didn't own a car, this is how much you'd be saving each month.		
Retirement Savings - If you didn't own a car and began investing your monthly automobile savings at age 25 at 5% interest, you would have this amount by the time you retired (if you retired at age 67).	$ 1,308,896.50	$ 941,099.15
College Savings - If you didn't own a car and invested your monthly automobile savings for 18 years at 5% interest, you'd have this amount for your children's college education.	$ 267,081.34	$ 192,032.01
Home Mortgage - If you didn't own a car and bought a house using your monthly automobile savings, you could obtain this home mortgage, assuming a 5% fixed, 30-year loan.	$ 142,474.39 This would be enough to cover 84.4% of the purchase price of the median existing home in the US in Dec 2010.	$ 102,439.36 This would be enough to cover 60.68% of the purchase price of the median existing home in the US in Dec 2010.

Your Rights as a Consumer

You have rights as a consumer. Your rights come from laws governing various kinds of transactions. Knowing your rights can help you avoid problems in the first place, save you money and hassle or help you to get compensation.

The Basics:

- Always read contracts carefully and completely before signing. If you have questions or concerns, don't sign until you are satisfied with answers from the seller.

- Be cautious about ads promising guaranteed jobs, guaranteed loans, credit repair, debt consolidation or similar claims. Many of these offers are only a way to get you to send money in advance in exchange for little or no service.

- Don't be pressured into buying. If you're not sure, take some time to think about it.

- Protect your personal information by only revealing what is absolutely necessary. People who obtain very basic personal information about you can drain your bank accounts or charge things to your credit cards. They could also bombard you with unwanted solicitations and marketing.

- When shopping online, know the following before you commit to paying: Who are you dealing with? Exactly what you are buying? What you are agreeing to? How much you are paying? How the payment system is secured? And what information you are giving to the vendor and why?

- Ask about the seller's refund or exchange policy before you buy. While no legal obligation exists for businesses to accept returned items unless they are defective, it is generally accepted that offering refunds or exchanges is a critical part of developing and maintaining good customer relations.

- Always check the warranty on a product before you buy it. A warranty is a written guarantee to the purchaser of an item promising to replace or repair the article, if necessary, within a specified period.

How to Complain Effectively

When I encounter unsatisfactory services or products, I just chalk it up as a learning experience. Why should I complain?

Legitimate complaints help everybody in the marketplace. Complaints help prevent inferior products and ineffective policies in the marketplace. They also alert businesses to product quality, service and distribution problems.

How long after the incident should I issue my complaint?

The sooner, the better! There are legal time limits, depending on the situation, so act quickly.

Who should I direct my complaint to?

Always go to the seller first. All good businesses recognize a valid complaint as an opportunity rather than a bother. Be sure you are dealing with someone who has the authority to rectify the problem.

How can I complain effectively?

It is important to clearly identify the problem. You need to explain why you are dissatisfied and what you would like done to correct the problem.

Make sure you have proof of payment or proof of dealings with the business. Make copies of receipts, cancelled checks, guarantees and any other correspondence between yourself and the business. Never give away the original copy.

The best approach is to be polite but firm. Do not lose your temper. Be persistent. Do not give up until you feel you have received a satisfactory response.

It is important that you be reasonable and fair. You should determine the business's refund policy before making any purchases and ensure that you have properly complied with the terms and warranties. You have no legal right for a refund unless the goods are defective.

What should I do if the seller refuses to recognize my complaint?

When dealing with the seller fails, you may want to take your complaint to the next level. If you are complaining about product quality, the next step is to complain to the manufacturer. If the business belongs to a professional organization or association, the association may be willing to assist you with your problem. Otherwise, you may have to consider utilizing legal action to resolve your concerns or contact one of the following organizations for assistance.

1. **State Consumer Protection Office**

    These institutions administer laws governing business practices, consumer product warranties, internet transactions, auctioneers, cemeteries, charitable fund-raising businesses, collection agents, credit reporting agencies, direct sellers, car dealers, sellers of training courses, video outlets and film classifications. You can find the branch for your region at http://www.usa.gov/directory/stateconsumer/index.shtml.

2. **Better Business Bureau of you state or region.**

    The Better Business Bureau collects and reports information to help prospective buyers make informed decisions in dealing with both businesses and charitable organizations. The Better Business Bureau facilitates communication between the company and the consumer to help both sides come to a satisfactory resolution of the complaint.

3. **Trade Associations**

    Contact trade associations to help solve problems between their member companies and consumers. Many of them also provide consumer information online and through publications. An alphabetical list can be found at http://www.usa.gov/directory/tradeassc/index.shtml.

4. **Small Claims Court**

If you feel that you need to hire an attorney or take your complaint to Small Claims Court, you can find both at this link: http://www.usa.gov/topics/consumer/complaint/legal.shtml.

Tips for Filing a Complaint

When filing a complaint, keep these things in mind:

- Remain calm. The person who can help didn't cause the problem.

- Don't use an angry, threatening or sarcastic tone.

- State exactly what you want done about the problem.

- Document each step, and keep copies.

- Start with the seller first. You can resolve many problems by calling a company's toll free number. Even on the phone, you should know the details of the complaint. You can use the sample letter below to jot down a few notes before you call. If necessary, ask to speak to a manager.

- If that doesn't work, send a letter or e-mail to the manufacturer's national headquarters or consumer affairs office. Some experts suggest that a letter is the most effective method for contacting a company. If e-mails and phone calls don't work, try the old fashioned way.

Complaint Checklist

Before you complain, ask yourself the following questions. They will help you decide if your complaint is valid.

1. Did you gather information about the product before purchasing it to make sure that the product would serve your purpose?

2. Did you fully explain to the store staff what you wanted the product for?

3. Did you use the product only for the purpose described?

4. Did you examine the quality of the product before you purchased it?

5. Did you follow the instructions for the assembly, use and care of the product?

6. Are you unhappy with the product because it is a different size or color than what you ordered?

7. Are you unhappy with the product because there are parts missing?

8. Are you unhappy with the product because it was delivered to you damaged or broken or it didn't last very long?

9. Are you unhappy with the product because it does not match the description or sample?

10. Are you unhappy with the product because you changed your mind about the color, size or model you wanted?

You have a valid complaint if you answered:

- "Yes" to questions 1-5

- "Yes" to one of questions 6-9

- "No" to question 10

Sample Complaint Letter

Use the sample complaint (courtesy www.usa.gov) below to draft a complaint letter or e-mail. You can also copy and paste your complaint into a company's "Contact Us" form.

Your Address
Your City, State, ZIP
(Your e-mail address if sending via e-mail)

Date

Name of Contact Person (if available)
Title (if available)
Company Name
Consumer Complaint Division (if you have no specific contact)
Street Address
City, State, Zip Code

Dear **(Contact Person):**

Re: **(account number, if applicable)**

On **(date)**, I **(bought, leased, rented, or had repaired)** a **(name of the product, with serial or model number or service performed)** at **(location, date and other important details of the transaction)**.

Unfortunately, your product **(or service)** has not performed well **(or the service was inadequate)** because **(state the problem)**. I am disappointed because **(explain the problem: for example, the product does not work properly, the service was not performed correctly, I was billed the wrong amount, something was not disclosed clearly or was misrepresented, etc.)**.

To resolve the problem, I would appreciate your **(state the specific action you want - money back, charge card credit, repair, exchange, etc.)**. Enclosed are copies **(do not send originals)** of my records **(include receipts, guarantees, warranties, canceled checks, contracts, model and serial numbers, and any other documents)**.

I look forward to your reply and a resolution to my problem and will wait until **(set a time limit)** before seeking help from a consumer protection agency or the Better Business Bureau. Please contact me at the above address or by phone at **(home and/or office numbers with area code)**.

Sincerely,

Your name

Enclosure(s)

Remember to:

- describe purchase
- include the name of product, serial number
- include the date and place of purchase
- state problem
- give history
- ask for specific action
- allow time for action
- state how you can be reached
- enclose copies of documents (but never send originals)
- Keep copies of all your letters, faxes, e-mails, and related documents.

Back to School

"It isn't what the book costs.
It's what it will cost you if you don't read it."
- Jim Rohn

It's no secret that going back to school either part-time or full-time could increase your future earning power. It can be one of the greatest investments that you make in yourself. However, school can be expensive. How can you finance it?

High School Equivalency

If you have not completed high school and you would like to as an adult, you can write an exam called the GED that will earn you your diploma upon passing. The GED Tests are a set of five tests in the core high school curriculum areas:

Language Arts, Reading: 65 minutes
Language Arts, Writing: 120 minutes
Mathematics: 90 minutes
Science: 80 minutes
Social Studies: 70 minutes

The examinee **must pass each subtest** with a minimum score of **four hundred and ten (410) points** and a minimum **total score** of **2250 points**. If the examinee does not pass a subtest the first time, the examinee may retest two more times, with a total of three opportunities per contract year. If the examinee passes all of the tests but does not earn the minimum 2250 points to pass the overall exam, the examinee may retest any one of the five tests in an effort to reach 2250 points.

The cost of writing the GED Tests varies in each state from $7.50 - $150.00. Check with your state GED Administrator.

Passing the GED tests may require some preparation on your part. Some people prepare intensively by taking classes or studying GED preparation books and other materials. Others are comfortable with simply brushing up on a few of the subject areas where they feel they need practice. There are books that specialize in the American GED preparation. As well there are prep courses. Note: GED preparation services are **not** regulated in many states so be careful about which you choose. Your local YMCA sometimes provides pre-tests for free to see how ready you are for the exam and also provide preparation for the actual exam. You can find a list of training options for your location on the internet.

For more information, go to this website: http://www.gedtestingservice.com

Student Financial Assistance

If you want to attend a postsecondary institution, but need financial help, you may qualify for financial assistance through your state government. Check your state's website for details.

The Free Application for Federal Student Aid (known as the FAFSA) is a form that can be prepared annually by current and prospective college students (undergraduate and graduate) to determine their eligibility for student financial aid (including the Pell Grant, Federal student loans and Federal Work-Study).

Despite its name, the application is not for a single federal program, being rather the gateway of consideration for:
- the nine federal student-aid programs
- the 605 state aid programs
- most of the institutional aid available

The U.S. Department of Education begins accepting the application beginning January 1 of each year for the upcoming academic year. Each application period is 18 months; most federal, state, and institutional aid is provided on a first come, first served basis. Students are advised to submit a FAFSA as early as possible for consideration for maximum financial assistance.

The Department of Education recommends you utilize the IRS Data Retrieval Tool (DRT), which is made available on the FAFSA. This tool will retrieve most of your tax information, excluding wages, directly from the IRS and automatically input the information on your application. The DRT can be used for students and parents.

The FAFSA consists of numerous questions (at least 130 for the 2010–2011 academic year) regarding a student's (and his or her family's) assets, income, and dependency. These are entered into a formula that determines the Expected Family Contribution (EFC). A number of factors are used in determining the EFC including the household size, income, number of students from household in college and assets (not including retirement and 401(k) funds). This information is required because of the expectation that parents will contribute to their child's education, whether that is true or not.

A Student Aid Report (SAR), which is a summary of the FAFSA responses, is forwarded to the student. The student should review the SAR carefully for errors and make any corrections. An electronic version of the SAR (called an ISIR) is made available to the colleges/universities the student selects on the FAFSA. The ISIR is also sent to state agencies that award need-based aid.

Some colleges also require the CSS Profile to be filled out as early as the same deadline as an early admissions or early decision application deadline. The CSS is a fee-based product of the College Board and usually concerns funds disbursed by a college rather than federal funds.

Nearly every student is eligible for some form of financial aid. Students who may not be eligible for need-based aid may still be eligible for an unsubsidized Stafford Loan regardless of income or circumstances.

A student who can meet the following criteria may be eligible for aid:

- is a U.S. citizen, a U.S. national, or an eligible non-citizen;
- has a valid Social Security number;
- has a high school diploma or GED;
- is registered with the U.S. Selective Service (male students age 18–25);
- completes a FAFSA promising to use any federal aid for education purposes;
- does not owe refunds on any federal student grants;

- is not in default on any student loans; and
- has not been found guilty of the sale or possession of illegal drugs while federal aid was being received.

Student Aid and Fiscal Responsibility Act (SAFRA) changes the criteria for suspension of eligibility for drug-related offenses. Previously, students could lose eligibility for either the possession or sale of a controlled substance during the period of enrollment. SAFRA drops the penalties for possession of a controlled substance but retains the penalties for sale of a controlled substance. SAFRA increases the suspension to two years for a first offense and indefinite for a second offense.

FAFSA has several different types of financial aid. The four most common types of aid:

- Pell Grant – A grant of up to $5,550 for students with low EFCs.
- Stafford Loans – A loan with interest set at 6.8%. If subsidized, the interest is paid by the government while the student is enrolled at least half time. If unsubsidized, the interest accumulates onto the outstanding balance.
- Perkins Loans – A loan that is like the Stafford but is lent directly by schools that are Title IV-eligible.
- The Federal Work-Study Program – A program where students can get part-time work, up to a certain amount, and have 75% of their wages reimbursed by the federal government.

Other ways to help finance your education:

Tax Credits for Higher Education Expenses

Two tax credits help offset the costs (tuition, fees, books, supplies, equipment) of college or career school by reducing the amount of your income tax:

- The American Opportunity Credit allows you to claim up to $2,500 per student per year for the first four years of school as the student works toward a degree or similar credential.

- The Lifetime Learning Credit allows you to claim up to $2,000 per student per year for any college or career school tuition and fees, as well as for books, supplies, and equipment that were required for the course and had to be purchased from the school.

Even if you normally wouldn't file a tax return because your income level is low, you should still do it. If you don't, you will miss out on tax credits that could put money in your pocket.

Student Loan Interest Deduction

You can take a tax deduction for the interest paid on student loans that you took out for yourself, your spouse, or a dependent. This benefit applies to all loans (not just federal student loans) used to pay for higher education expenses. The maximum deduction is $2,500 a year.

Coverdell Education Savings Account

A Coverdell Education Savings Account allows up to $2,000 a year to be put aside for a student's education expenses (elementary, secondary, or college). (Discussed earlier in this book.)

Qualified Tuition Programs (QTPs; also known as 529 Plans)

A QTP/529 plan is established by a state or school so that you can either prepay or save up to pay education-related expenses. Once you're in college or career school and you withdraw money from your account to pay your education expenses, the money you withdraw will not be taxed. Learn more about state 529 plans. To find out whether the college you plan to attend participates in a QTP, ask the financial aid or admissions staff. (Discussed earlier in this book.)

Federal Work-Study Jobs to Help Pay For College

Federal Work-Study provides part-time jobs for undergraduate and graduate students with financial need, allowing them to earn money to help pay education expenses. The program encourages community service work and work related to the student's course of study.

Here's a quick overview of Federal Work-Study:

- It provides part-time employment while you are enrolled in school.

- It's available to undergraduate, graduate, and professional students with financial need.

- It's available to full-time or part-time students.

- It's administered by schools participating in the Federal Work-Study Program. Check with your school's financial aid office to find out if your school participates.

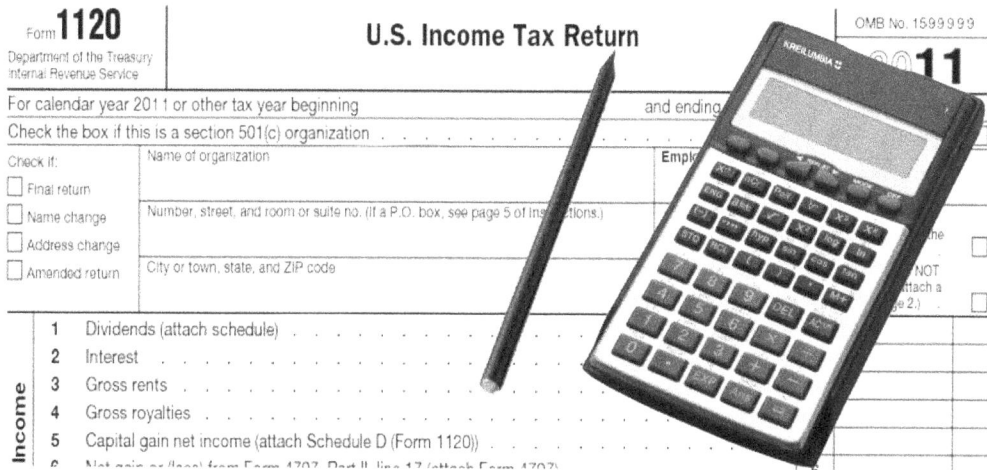

$\mathbf{P}$reparing Your Tax Return

"Today, it takes more brains and effort to make out the income-tax form than it does to make the income."
– Alfred E. Neuman

Have you paid your income taxes yet? A tax return is basically your report to the government of all of your income and some other financial details for a given year. While your return may show that you have to pay more tax, you may also be eligible for a tax refund if you have credits for expenses like health care, child care or school. Before you begin, take some time to learn more about taxes and filing a tax return.

- For information about taxation, contact the Internal Revenue Service (IRS). http://www.irs.gov

- Income tax is collected by the IRS on behalf of the federal and state governments. Be aware of the deadline for filing your tax return: April 15th. There are financial penalties for filing a late return if you owe the government money.

- Keep a record of your income from all sources. If you work for someone else, they are obligated to send you a statement listing your income and any deductions that have been made for income taxes, Medicare, Social Security, etc. Use this information to fill out your tax return.

- You can fill out and send your tax return on paper or electronically. Print forms are available from several sources:

  - **On the Internet:** You can view and print the required forms online, or you can download the files onto your computer's hard drive at irs.gov.

  - **By phone:** You can get a printed copy of the materials mailed to you by calling 1-800-TAX-FORM (1-800-829-3676).

  - **In-person:** You can get the forms and instructions for your state from any IRS local office, post office or library near you between February and early May each year.

- To file your return over the Internet via IRS's E-FILE service, you will need to purchase an IRS-approved tax filing software or use the IRS's online fillable forms or have your return filed by a professional tax service. The benefit of this method of reporting is that, if the government owes you a refund, you will probably receive it within 2-3 weeks.

- If you send in a paper form, include your information slips detailing your sources of income and deductions.

- Keep a copy, paper or electronic, of your return for future reference.

Do I have to file a tax return if I made under $9,350?

You do not but you may want to file one if your employer deducted income tax from your pay checks. As you would not be required to pay tax for that amount of income, you may be entitled to a refund of the income tax deducted.

College students that file their tax returns are in better shape for financial aid purposes than students that do not file a tax return. Filing a tax return indicates if the student has any bank accounts that earn interest and dividends or investment accounts that hold stock. It can also be used to claim financial independence from parents.

Filing an income tax return helps establish an individual's earnings history. The IRS forwards tax returns to the Social Security Administration where it is used to calculate social security benefits.

Certain credits and government stimulus payments are available to individuals even if they did not work and had no income tax withholding. However, the individual must have a tax return on file to be eligible. When the government announces a stimulus payment, it is often too late to go back and file a tax return for the prior year without incurring a late filing penalty fee.

Do I have to include any cash tips as income?

All tips you receive are income, and subject to income tax. This includes tips customers give you directly, tips customers charge on credit cards that your employer gives you, and your share of tips split with other employees. The following are some examples of tips:

- A customer leaves money on the table at the end of the meal and the server keeps the whole amount;

- A customer gives a tip directly to a bellhop, door person, car attendant, hair stylist etc.;

- Tips pooled and/or shared among employees;

- When paying the bill by credit card, a customer includes an amount for a tip on the credit card and the employer returns the tip amount in cash to the employee;

- When paying the bill by debit card, a customer includes an amount for a tip and the employer returns the tip amount in cash to the employee;

Is my scholarship or fellowship money taxable?

If you received a scholarship or fellowship, all or part of it may be taxable, even if you did not receive a Form W-2. Generally, the entire amount is taxable if you are not a candidate for a degree.

If you are a candidate for a degree, you generally can exclude from income that part of the grant used for:

- Tuition and fees required for enrollment or attendance, or
- Fees, books, supplies, and equipment required for your courses.

You cannot exclude from income any part of the grant used for other purposes, such as room and board.

A *scholarship* generally is an amount paid for the benefit of a student at an educational institution to aid in the pursuit of studies. The student may be in either a graduate or an undergraduate program.

A *fellowship* grant generally is an amount paid for the benefit of an individual to aid in the pursuit of study or research.

Example 1

Alia receives a $5,000 fellowship grant that is not designated for any specific use. Alia is a degree candidate. She spends $4,500 for tuition and $500 for her personal expenses. Alia is required to include $500 in income.

Example 2

Michael, a degree candidate, receives a $3,000 scholarship, with $2,000 specifically designated for tuition and $1,000 specifically designated for living expenses. His tuition is $2,600. He may exclude $2,000 from income which was designated for tuition, but the other $1,000 designated for living expenses is taxable and must be included in income.

Pell Grants, Supplemental Educational Opportunity Grants, and Grants to States for State Student Incentives.

These grants are non-taxable scholarships to the extent used for tuition and course-related expenses during the grant period.

Reduced Tuition

You may be entitled to reduced tuition because you or one of your parents was an employee of the school. If so, the amount of the reduction is not taxable so long as the tuition is for education below the graduate level. The reduced tuition is taxable if it represents payment for your services.

Graduate Student Exception

Tax-free treatment of reduced tuition can also apply to a graduate student who performs teaching or research activities at an educational institution. The qualified tuition reduction must be for education furnished by that institution and not represent payment for services.

Contest prizes

Scholarship prizes won in a contest are not scholarships or fellowships if you do not have to use the prizes for your education. If you can use the prize for any purpose, the entire amount is taxable.

Qualified State Tuition Program

If you receive money from a qualified state tuition program, only the amount that is more than the amount contributed to the program is taxable. Other benefits are partly a non-taxable return of the contributions made to the program on your behalf (for example, by your parents).

If you don't feel that you comfortable filing out the tax forms manually or using tax software, there are some tax preparers that will offer a discount for students. Just be sure that the preparer is reputable and will stand by you in case the Internal Revenue Service requests an audit.

"Accept responsibility for your life. Know that it is you who will get you where you want to go, no one else."
– Les Brown

APPENDIX A: Consumer Protection Agencies

Alabama
Alabama Office of the Attorney General
Consumer Affairs Section
501 Washington Ave.
Montgomery, AL 36104
1-800-392-5658
Website: http://www.alabama.gov/portal/secondary.jsp?id=consumerProtection

Alaska
Office of the Attorney General
Consumer Protection Unit
1031 W. 4th Ave., Suite 200
Anchorage, AK 99501-5903
1-888-576-2529
Email: consumerprotection@alaska.gov
Website: http://www.law.state.ak.us/department/civil/consumer/cpindex.html

Arizona
Arizona Office of the Attorney General-Phoenix
Consumer Information and Complaints
1275 W. Washington St.
Phoenix, AZ 85007
1-800-352-8431
Email: consumerinfo@azag.gov
Website: http://www.azag.gov/

Arkansas
Arkansas Office of the Attorney General
Consumer Protection Division
323 Center St., Suite 200
Little Rock, AR 72201
1-800-482-8982
Website: http://www.arkansasag.gov/

California
California Department of Consumer Affairs
Consumer Information Division
1625 N. Market Blvd., Suite N 112
Sacramento, CA 95834
1-800-952-5210
Email: dca@dca.ca.gov
Website: www.dca.ca.gov

Colorado
Colorado Office of the Attorney General
Consumer Protection Division
1525 Sherman St., 7th Floor
Denver, CO 80203
1-800-222-4444
Email: stop.fraud@state.co.us
Website: www.coloradoattorneygeneral.gov

Connecticut
Department of Consumer Protection
165 Capitol Ave.
Hartford, CT 06106-1630
1-800-842-2649
Email: dcp.tpd@ct.gov
Website: www.ct.gov/dcp

Delaware
Delaware Department of Justice
Consumer Protection Division
820 N. French St., 5th Floor
Wilmington, DE 19801
1-800-220-5424
Email: consumer.protection@state.de.us
Website: www.attorneygeneral.delaware.gov

District of Columbia
Department of Consumer and Regulatory Affairs
1100 4th St., SW
Washington, DC 20024
202-442-4400
Email: dcra@dc.gov
Website: www.drca.dc.gov

Florida
Florida Office of the Attorney General
PL-01 The Capitol
Tallahassee, FL 32399-1050
1-866-966-7226
Website: www.myfloridalegal.com

Georgia
Georgia Governors Office of Consumer Affairs
2 Martin Luther King, Jr. Dr., SE
Suite 356
Atlanta, GA 30334-9077
404-651-8600
Website: www.consumer.georgia.gov

Hawaii
Hawaii Department of Commerce and Consumer Affairs - Honolulu (Main Location)
Office of Consumer Protection
235 S. Beretania St., Suite 801
Honolulu, HI 96813
808-587-3222
Email: ocp@dcca.hawaii.gov
Website: www.hawaii.gov/dcca/ocp

Idaho
Idaho Attorney General's Office
Consumer Protection Division
954 W. Jefferson, 2nd Floor
PO Box 83720
Boise, ID 83720
1-800-432-3545
Website: www.ag.idaho.gov

Illinois
Illinois Office of the Attorney General -Chicago
Consumer Fraud Bureau
100 W. Randolph St.
Chicago, IL 60601
1-800-386-5438
Website: www.illinoisattorneygeneral.gov

Indiana
Office of the Attorney General
Consumer Protection Division
Government Center South, 5th Floor
302 W. Washington St.
Indianapolis, IN 46204
1-800-382-5516
Website: www.indianaconsumer.com

Iowa
Iowa Office of the Attorney General
Consumer Protection Division
1305 E. Walnut St.
Des Moines, IA 50319
1-888-777-4590
Email: consumer@ag.state.ia.us
Website: www.iowaattorneygeneral.org

Kansas

Office of Kansas Attorney
Consumer Protection and Antitrust Division
120 S.W. 10th St., Suite 430
Topeka, KS 66612-1597
1-800-432-2310
Website: www.ag.ks.gov

Kentucky

Kentucky Office of the Attorney General
Consumer Protection Division
1024 Capital Center Dr.
Frankfort, KY 40601
1-888-432-9257
Email: consumer.protection@ag.ky.gov
Website: www.ag.ky.gov/cp

Louisiana

Louisiana Office of the Attorney General
Consumer Protection Section
1885 N. 3rd St.
Baton Rouge, LA 70802
1-800-351-4889
Email: ConsumerInfo@ag.state.la.us
Website: www.ag.state.la.us

Maine

Bureau of Consumer Credit Protection
35 State House Station
Augusta, ME 04333
1-800-332-8529
Website: www.credit.maine.gov

Maryland

Maryland Office of the Attorney General
Consumer Protection Division
200 Saint Paul Pl.
Baltimore, MD 21202
1-888-743-0023
Email: consumer@oag.state.md.us
Website: http://www.oag.state.md.us/consumer/

Massachusetts

Office of Consumer Affairs and Business Regulation
10 Park Plaza, Suite 5170
Boston, MA 02116
1-888-283-3757
Website: www.mass.gov/consumer

Michigan
Office of the Attorney General
Consumer Protection Division
PO Box 30213
Lansing, MI 48909-7713
1-877-765-8388
Website: www.michigan.gov/ag

Minnesota
Office of the Attorney General
Consumer Services Division
1400 Bremer Tower
445 Minnesota St.
St. Paul, MN 55101
1-800-657-3787
Website: www.ag.state.mn.us

Mississippi
Mississippi Office of the Attorney General
Consumer Protection Division
PO Box 22947
Jackson, MS 39225-2947
1-800-281-4418
Website: www.ago.state.ms.us

Missouri
Missouri Attorney General's Office
Consumer Protection Unit
PO Box 899
Jefferson City, MO 65102
1-800-392-8222
Email: consumer.help@ago.mo.gov
Website: www.ago.mo.gov

Montana
Montana Office of Consumer Protection
Office of Consumer Protection
2225 11th Ave.
PO Box 200151
Helena, MT 59620-0151
1-800-481-6896
Email: contactocp@mt.gov
Website: www.doj.mt.gov/consumer

Nebraska

Nebraska Office of the Attorney General
Consumer Protection Division
2115 State Capitol
Lincoln, NE 68509
1-800-727-6432
Email: ago.consumer@nebraska.gov
Website: www.ago.ne.gov

Nevada

Website: www.fightfraud.nv.gov

New Hampshire

New Hampshire Office of the Attorney General
Consumer Protection and Antitrust Bureau
33 Capitol St.
Concord, NH 03301
1-888-468-4454
Email: DOJ-CPB@doj.nh.gov
Website: www.doj.nh.gov/consumer

New Jersey

Department of Law and Public Safety
Division of Consumer Affairs
124 Halsey St.
Newark, NJ 07102
1-800-242-5846
Email: askconsumeraffairs@lps.state.nj.us
Website: www.njconsumeraffairs.gov

New Mexico

Office of Attorney General
Consumer Protection Division
PO Drawer 1508
Santa Fe, NM 87504-1508
1-800-678-1508
Website: www.nmag.gov

New York

New York State Department of State
Division of Consumer Protection
Consumer Assistance Unit
99 Washington Ave.
Albany, NY 12231
1-800-697-1220
Website: www.nysconsumer.gov

North Carolina
North Carolina Department of Agriculture and Consumer Services
1001 Mail Service Center
Raleigh, NC 27699-1001
919-707-3000
Website: www.ncagr.gov/

North Dakota
Office of the Attorney General
Consumer Protection and Antitrust Division
Gateway Professional Center
1050 E. Interstate Ave., Suite 200
Bismarck, ND 58503-5574
1-800-472-2600
Email: ndag@nd.gov
Website: www.ag.nd.gov

Ohio
Ohio Attorney General's Office
Consumer Protection Section
30 E. Broad St., 14th Floor
Columbus, OH 43215-3400
1-800-282-0515
Website: www.ohioattorneygeneral.gov

Oklahoma
Oklahoma Attorney General
Consumer Protection Unit
313 N.E. 21st St.
Oklahoma City, OK 73105
Website: www.oag.ok.gov

Oregon
Oregon Department of Justice
Financial Fraud/Consumer Protection Section
1162 Court St., NE
Salem, OR 97301-4096
1-877-877-9392
Email: consumer.hotline@doj.state.or.us
Website: www.doj.state.or.us

Pennsylvania
Office of the Attorney General
Bureau of Consumer Protection
Strawberry Square, 14th Floor
Harrisburg, PA 17120
1-800-441-2555
Website: www.attorneygeneral.gov

Rhode Island
Rhode Island Department of the Attorney General
Consumer Protection Unit
150 S. Main St.
Providence, RI 02903
401-274-4400
Email: contactus@riag.ri.gov
Website: www.riag.state.ri.us

South Carolina
South Carolina Department of Consumer Affairs
PO Box 5757
Columbia, SC 29250
1-800-922-1594
Email: scdca@scconsumer.gov
Website: www.scconsumer.gov

South Dakota
South Dakota Office of the Attorney General
Consumer Protection
1302 E. Hwy. 14, Suite 3
Pierre, SD 57501
1-800-300-1986
Email: consumerhelp@state.sd.us
Website: www.state.sd.us/atg

Tennessee
Tennessee Department of Commerce and Insurance
Division of Consumer Affairs
500 James Robertson Pkwy., 12th Floor
Nashville, TN 37243-0600
1-800-342-8385
Email: consumer.affairs@tn.gov
Website: www.tn.gov/consumer

Texas
Texas Office of the Attorney General
Consumer Protection Division
PO Box 12548
Austin, TX 78711-2548
1-800-621-0508
Website: www.oag.state.tx.us

Utah
Utah Department of Commerce
Division of Consumer Protection
160 E. 300 S, 2nd Floor
PO Box 146704
Salt Lake City, UT 84114-6704
1-800-721-7233
Email: consumerprotection@utah.gov
Website: www.consumerprotection.utah.gov

Vermont
Vermont Office of the Attorney General
Consumer Assistance Program
146 University Pl.
Burlington, VT 05405
1-800-649-2424
Email: consumer@uvm.edu
Website: www.atg.state.vt.us

Vermont
Virginia Office of the Attorney General
Consumer Protection Section
900 E. Main St.
Richmond, VA 23219
1-800-552-9963
Website: www.ag.viriginia.gov

Washington
Washington Office of the Attorney General
Consumer Protection Division
PO Box 40100
1125 Washington St., SE
Olympia, WA 98504-0100
1-800-833-6384
Website: www.atg.wa.gov

West Virginia
Office of the Attorney General
Consumer Protection Division
PO Box 1789
Charleston, WV 25326-1789
1-800-368-8808
Email: consumer@wvago.gov
Website: www.wvago.gov

Wisconsin
Wisconsin Department of Agriculture, Trade and Consumer Protection
Bureau of Consumer Protection
PO Box 8911
2811 Agriculture Dr.
Madison, WI 53708-8911
1-800-422-7128
Email: DATCPhotline@wi.gov
Website: www.datcp.state.wi.us

Wyoming
Office of the Attorney General
Consumer Protection Unit
123 State Capitol
200 W. 24th St.
Cheyenne, WY 82002
307-777-5833
Website: www.attorneygeneral.state.wy.us

APPENDIX B: State Grants

Federal: http://studentaid.ed.gov/types

Alabama: http://www.ache.alabama.gov/StudentAsst/Programs.htm

Alaska: https://akadvantage.alaska.gov/Grants_and_Scholarships.aspx

Arizona http://azhighered.gov/

Arkansas: http://www.adhe.edu/divisions/financialaid/Pages/fa_acs.aspx

California: http://www.csac.ca.gov/

Colorado: http://highered.colorado.gov/Finance/FinancialAid/TypesofStateAidAvailable.html

Connecticut: http://www.ctohe.org/SFA/default.shtml

Delaware: http://www.doe.k12.de.us/infosuites/students_family/dheo/how_to_apply/financial_aid/default.shtml

DC: http://osse.dc.gov/service/higher-education-financial-services

Florida: http://www.floridastudentfinancialaid.org/SSFAD/home/ProgramsOffered.htm

Georgia: https://secure.gacollege411.org/Financial_Aid_Planning/_default.aspx

Hawaii: http://westoahu.hawaii.edu/grants

Idaho: http://www.boardofed.idaho.gov/scholarship/scholarship_jump.asp

Illinois: http://www.isac.org/students/during-college/types-of-financial-aid/grants/

Indiana: http://in.gov/ssaci/2335.htm

Iowa: http://www.iowacollegeaid.gov/ScholarshipsGrants/scholarshipsgrants.html

Kansas: http://financialaid.ku.edu/programs/

Kentucky: http://www.kheaa.com/website/kheaa/cap?main=1

Louisiana: http://www.osfa.state.la.us/SandG.htm

Maine: http://www.maine.gov/education/highered/FinancialAid/FinancialAid.htm

Maryland: http://www.mhec.state.md.us/

Massachusetts: http://www.osfa.mass.edu/default.asp?page=aidPrograms

Michigan: http://www.michigan.gov/mistudentaid

Minnesota: http://www.getreadyforcollege.org/grIndex.cfm

Mississippi: http://www.mississippi.edu/riseupms/financialaid.php

Missouri: http://dhe.mo.gov/ppc/grants/

Montana: http://www.mus.edu/Prepare/Pay/Types_Of_Aid.asp

Nebraska: http://www.ccpe.state.ne.us/PublicDoc/Ccpe/financialaid.asp

Nevada: http://financialaid.unlv.edu/Information/Grants/index.asp

New Hampshire: http://www.education.nh.gov/highered/finanical/index.htm

New Jersey: http://www.hesaa.org/Pages/GrantsandScholarshipsDetails.aspx

New Mexico: http://hed.state.nm.us/Grants.aspx

New York: http://www.hesc.com/content.nsf/SFC/2/Grants_Scholarships_and_Awards

North Carolina: https://www.cfnc.org/paying/schol/info_schol.jsp

North Dakota: http://www.ndus.edu/students/paying-for-college/grants-scholarships/

Ohio: http://www.ohiohighered.org/sgs

Oklahoma: http://www.okcollegestart.org/Financial_Aid/Types_of_Aid/_default.aspx

Oregon: http://www.oregonstudentaid.gov/financial-aid.aspx

Pennsylvania: http://www.pheaa.org/funding-opportunities/index.shtml

Rhode Island: http://www.riheaa.org/sng/sg_elig_reqs.php

South Carolina: http://www.che.sc.gov/New_Web/GoingToCollege/FinAsst.htm

South Dakota: http://sdos.sdbor.edu/

Tennessee: http://www.tn.gov/collegepays//mon_college/grants.htm

Texas: www.collegeforalltexans.com

Utah: http://www.higheredutah.org/scholarship_info/

Vermont: http://services.vsac.org/wps/wcm/connect/vsac/VSAC

Virginia: http://www.schev.edu/students/undergradFinancialaidPrograms.asp

Washington: http://www.sbctc.ctc.edu/college/s_opportunitygrants.aspx

West Virginia: http://wvhepcnew.wvnet.edu/index.php

Wisconsin: http://heab.state.wi.us/programs.html

Wyoming: http://edu.wyoming.gov/Programs/grants.aspx

APPENDIX C: State Agencies for Financial Assistance

Alabama
Alabama Commission on Higher Education
Office of Student Assistance
P.O. Box 302000
Montgomery, AL 36130-2000
Phone: (334) 242-2273
Email: cheryl.newton@ache.alabama.gov
Website: http://www.ache.alabama.gov/StudentAsst/Index.htm

Kentucky Higher Education Assistance Authority
P.O. Box 798
Frankfort, KY 40602-0798
Toll-Free: (800) 928-8926
Email: grants@kheaa.com
Website: http://www.kheaa.com/
States Served: Alabama, Kentucky

Alaska
Alaska Commission on Postsecondary Education
P.O. Box 110505
Juneau, AK 99811-0505
Toll-Free: (800) 441-2962
Email: customer.service@alaska.gov
Website: http://akadvantage.alaska.gov

Arizona
Arizona Commission for Postsecondary Education
Suite 650
2020 North Central Avenue
Phoenix, AZ 85004
Phone: (602) 258-2435
Email: jsloan@azhighered.gov or cwilliams@azhighered.gov
Website: http://azhighered.gov/home.aspx

Arkansas
Arkansas Department of Higher Education
114 East Capitol Avenue
Little Rock, AR 72201
Toll-Free: (800) 547-8839
Email: taras@adhe.edu or stevef@adhe.edu
Website: http://www.adhe.edu/Pages/home.aspx

California
California Student Aid Commission
P.O. Box 419026
Rancho Cordova, CA 95741-9026
Toll-Free: (888) 224-7268
Email: studentsupport@csac.ca.gov
Website: http://www.csac.ca.gov/

Colorado
Colorado Department of Higher Education
Suite 16
1560 Broadway
Denver, CO 80202
Phone: (303) 866-2723
Email: executivedirector@dhe.state.co.us
Website: http://highered.colorado.gov/

Connecticut
Connecticut Department of Higher Education
61 Woodland Street
Hartford, CT 06105-2326
Phone: (860) 947-1855
Toll-Free: (800) 842-0229
Fax: (860) 947-1311
Email: sfa@ctdhe.org or mfrench@ctdhe.org
Website: http://www.ctdhe.org/

Delaware
Delaware Higher Education Commission
Carvel State Office Building
820 North French Street, 5F
Wilmington, DE 19801
Toll-Free: (800) 292-7935
Email: dhec@doe.k12.de.us or mlaffey@doe.k12.de.us
Website: http://www.doe.k12.de.us/dhec/

District of Columbia
Office of the State Superintendent of Education (District of Columbia)
State Board of Education
Suite 350 North
441 Fourth Street, NW
Washington, DC 20001
Phone: (202) 727-6436
Email: osse@dc.gov or sboe@dc.gov
Website: http://www.seo.dc.gov/

Florida

Office of Student Financial Assistance (Florida)
Florida Department of Education
325 West Gaines Street
Tallahassee, FL 32399-0400
Toll-Free: 800-366-3475
Email: OSFAStudentLoans@fldoe.org or OSFA@fldoe.org
Website: http://www.FloridaStudentFinancialAid.org

Georgia

Georgia Student Finance Commission
2082 East Exchange Place
Tucker, GA 30084
Toll-Free: (800) 505-4732
Email: monetr@gsfc.org or gsfcinfo@gsfc.org
Website: http://www.gsfc.org

Hawaii

No records found.

Idaho

Idaho State Board of Education
P.O. Box 83720
Boise, ID 83720-0037
Phone: (208) 332-1574
Email: dana.kelly@osbe.idaho.gov
Website: http://www.boardofed.idaho.gov/scholarships/index.asp

Illinois

Illinois Student Assistance Commission
1755 Lake Cook Road
Deerfield, IL 60015-5209
Toll-Free: (800) 899-4722
Email: collegezone@isac.org or dcalcara@isac.org
Website: http://www.collegezone.com/

Indiana

State Student Assistance Commission of Indiana
Suite 500
150 West Market Street
Indianapolis, IN 46204
Toll-Free: (888) 528-4719
Email: grants@ssaci.in.gov
Website: http://www.in.gov/ssaci/

Iowa
Iowa College Student Aid Commission
Fourth Floor
200 10th Street
Des Moines, IA 50309-3609
Toll-Free: (877)272-4456
Email: info@iowacollegeaid.org
Website: http://www.iowacollegeaid.org/

Kansas
Kansas Board of Regents (The)
Suite 520
1000 SW Jackson Street
Topeka, KS 66612-1368
Phone: (785) 296-3421
Email: dlindeman@ksbor.org or kstewart@ksbor.org
Website: http://www.kansasregents.org/financial_aid/index.html

Kentucky
Kentucky Higher Education Assistance Authority
P.O. Box 798
Frankfort, KY 40602-0798
Toll-Free: (800) 928-8926
Email: grants@kheaa.com
Website: http://www.kheaa.com/
States Served: Alabama, Kentucky

Louisiana
Louisiana Office of Student Financial Assistance
P.O. Box 91202
Baton Rouge, LA 70821-9202
Toll-Free: (800) 259-5626 x1012
Email: blavergne@osfa.la.gov or jrougeau@osfa.la.gov
Website: http://www.osfa.state.la.us/

Maine
Finance Authority of Maine
P.O. Box 949
Five Community Drive
Augusta, ME 04332-0949
Toll-Free: (800) 228-3734
Email: education@famemaine.com or info@famemaine.com
Website: http://www.famemaine.com/

Maryland

Maryland Higher Education Commission
Office of Student Financial Assistance
Suite 400
839 Bestgate Road
Annapolis, MD 21401
Toll-Free: (800) 974-0203
Email: osfamail@mhec.state.md.us or rparker@mhec.state.md.us
Website: http://www.mhec.state.md.us/financialAid/index.asp

Massachusetts

Office of Student Financial Assistance (Massachusetts)
State Department of Higher Education
Suite 200
454 Broadway
Revere, MA 02151
Phone: (617) 727-9420 x1313
Email: rdais@osfa.mass.edu or cmccurdy@osfa.mass.edu
Website: http://www.osfa.mass.edu/

Michigan

Michigan Higher Education Assistance Authority
Office of Scholarships and Grants
P.O. Box 30462
Lansing, MI 48909-7962
Toll-Free: (888) 447-2687
Email: osg@michigan.gov
Website: http://www.michigan.gov/osg

Minnesota

Minnesota Office of Higher Education
Suite 350
1450 Energy Park Drive
St. Paul, MN 55108-5227
Toll-Free: (800) 657-3866
Email: ginny.dodds@state.mn.us
Website: http://www.ohe.state.mn.us/index.cfm

Mississippi

Mississippi Office of Student Financial Aid
3825 Ridgewood Road
Jackson, MS 39211-6453
Toll-Free: (800) 327-2980
Email: sfa@ihl.state.ms.us or mcovington@mississippi.edu
Website: http://www.mississippi.edu/financialaid/

Missouri

Office of Student Financial Assistance (Missouri)
State Department of Higher Education
3515 Amazonas Drive
Jefferson City, MO 65109
Toll-Free: (800) 473-6757
Email: info@dhe.mo.gov or kelli.reed@dhe.mo.gov
Website: http://www.dhe.mo.gov/

Montana

Montana Guaranteed Student Loan Program
P.O. Box 203101
Helena, MT 59620-3101
Toll-Free: (800) 537-7508
Email: rmuffick@mgslp.state.mt.us
Website: http://www.mgslp.org/

Nebraska

Coordinating Commission for Postsecondary Education (Nebraska)
P.O. Box 95005
Suite 300
140 North Eighth Street
Lincoln, NE 68509-5005
Phone: (402) 471-2847
Email: ritchie.morrow@nebraska.gov or angela.dibbert@nebraska.gov
Website: http://www.ccpe.state.ne.us/PublicDoc/CCPE/Default.asp

Nevada

Nevada Commission on Postsecondary Education
Suite 202
3663 East Sunset Road
Las Vegas, NV 89120
Phone: (702) 486-7330
Email: bshanteler@cpe.state.nv.us or dperlman@cpe.state.nv.us
Website: http://www.cpe.state.nv.us/

New Hampshire

New Hampshire Postsecondary Education Commission
Suite 300
Three Barrell Court
Concord, NH 03301-8543
Phone: (603) 271-2555
Email: pedes@pec.state.nh.us
Website: http://www.state.nh.us/postsecondary/

New Jersey
New Jersey Higher Education Student Assistance Authority
P.O. Box 540
Trenton, NJ 08625
Toll-Free: (800) 792-8670
Email: amaglione@hesaa.org or fandrea@hesaa.org
Website: http://www.hesaa.org/

New Mexico
New Mexico Higher Education Department
2048 Galisteo Street
Santa Fe, NM 87505
Toll-Free: (800) 279-9777
Email: carlottam.abeyta@state.nm.us or suzanne.romero@state.nm.us
Website: http://www.nmhed.state.nm.us

New York
Higher Education Services Corporation (New York State)
99 Washington Avenue
Albany, NY 12255
Toll-Free: (888) 697-4372
Email: ngrose@hesc.org
Website: http://www.hesc.com/bulletin.nsf/

North Carolina
North Carolina State Education Assistance Authority
P.O. Box 13663
Research Triangle Park, NC 27709
Toll-Free: (866) 866-2362
Email: robbie@ncseaa.edu or information@ncseaa.edu
Website: http://www.CFNC.org

North Dakota
University System (North Dakota)
10th Floor, State Capitol
Department 215
600 East Boulevard Avenue
Bismark, ND 58505-0230
Phone: (701) 328-2960
Email: ndus.office@ndus.edu
Website: http://www.ndus.edu/

Ohio
Ohio Board of Regents
State Grants and Scholarships
36th Floor
30 East Broad Street
Columbus, OH 43215
Toll-Free: (888) 833-1133
Email: regents@regents.state.oh.us or cfoust@regents.state.oh.us
Website: http://regents.ohio.gov/

Oklahoma
Oklahoma State Regents for Higher Education
Suite 200
655 Research Parkway
Oklahoma City, OK 73104
Phone: (405) 225-9100
Email: rrichardson@osrhe.edu or studentinfo@osrhe.edu
Website: http://www.okhighered.org/

Oregon
No records found.

Pennsylvania
Pennsylvania Higher Education Assistance Agency
State Grants and Special Programs
1200 North Seventh Street
Harrisburg, PA 17102-1444
Toll-Free: (800) 692-7392
Email: granthelp@pheaa.org or cduzack@pheaa.org
Website: http://www.pheaa.org/

Rhode Island
Rhode Island Higher Education Assistance Authority
560 Jefferson Boulevard
Warwick, RI 02886
Toll-Free: (800) 922-9855
Email: grants@riheaa.org or info@riheaa.org
Website: http://www.riheaa.org/

South Carolina
South Carolina Higher Education Tuition Grants Commission
800 Dutch Square Boulevard
Suite 260A
Columbia, SC 29210
Phone: (803) 896-1120
Email: info@sctuitiongrants.org
Website: http://www.sctuitiongrants.com/

South Dakota

Office of Finance and Management (South Dakota)
State Department of Education
700 Governors Drive
Pierre, SD 57501
Phone: (605) 773-3248
Email: robyn.huffman@state.sd.us
Website: http://doe.sd.gov/

Tennessee

Tennessee Student Assistance Corporation
Suite 1510, Parkway Towers
404 James Robertson Parkway
Nashville, TN 37243-0820
Toll-Free: (800) 342-1663
Email: naomi.derryberry@state.tn.us
Website: http://www.tn.gov/CollegePays/index.html

Texas

Texas Higher Education Coordinating Board
P.O. Box 12788
Austin, TX 78711-2788
Toll-Free: (800) 242-3062
Email: grantinfo@thecb.state.tx.us
Website: http://www.thecb.state.tx.us/

Utah

Utah Higher Education Assistance Authority (UHEAA)
Board of Regents Building, The Gateway
60 South 400 West
Salt Lake City, UT 84101-1284
Toll-Free: (800) 418-8757
Email: uheaa@utahsbr.edu or mnemelka@utahsbr.edu
Website: http://www.uheaa.org/

Vermont

Vermont Student Assistance Corporation
P.O. Box 2000
10 East Allen Street
Winooski, VT 05404
Toll-Free: (800) 642-3177
Email: info@vsac.org
Website: http://www.vsac.org

Virginia

State Council of Higher Education for Virginia
101 North 14th Street
James Monroe Building, 10th Floor
Richmond, VA 23219
Phone: (804) 225-2600
Email: LeeAndes@schev.edu or MelissaCollumWyatt@schev.edu
Website: http://www.schev.edu/

Washington

Higher Education Coordinating Board (Washington)
917 Lakeridge Way SW
P.O. Box 43430
Olympia, WA 98504-3430
Phone: (360) 753-7800
Email: info@hecb.wa.gov or johnk@hecb.wa.gov
Website: http://www.hecb.wa.gov/

West Virginia

West Virginia Higher Education Policy Commission
Suite 700
1018 Kanawha Boulevard East
Charleston, WV 25301-2800
Phone: (304) 558-4614
Email: samples@hepc.wvnet.edu or canderson@hepc.wvnet.edu
Website: http://wvhepcnew.wvnet.edu/

Wisconsin

Wisconsin Higher Educational Aids Board
P.O. Box 7885
Madison, WI 53707-7885
Phone: (608) 267-2206
Email: HEABmail@wisconsin.gov or cassie.weisensel@wisconsin.gov
Website: http://heab.state.wi.us/

Wyoming

No records found.

APPENDIX D: Answers to Exercises

Income Tax Exercise:

1) $40,000 salary in Nevada

Federal:

	Up to $8,700 at 10%	Between $8,701 and $35,350 at 15%	Between $35,351 and $85,650 at 25%	Over $85,651 to $178,650 at 28%
Calculation	8700 * 0.10	(35350 - 8700) * 0.15	(40000 - 35350) * 0.25	N/A
Amount	$ 870.00 +	$ 3,997.50 +	$ 1,162.50 +	
Total Federal Tax	**$ 6,030.00**			

State (Nevada): No state tax

Total Income Tax in Nevada: $6,030.00

2) $70,000 salary in Virginia

Federal:

	Up to $8,700 at 10%	Between $8,701 and $35,350 at 15%	Between $35,351 and $85,650 at 25%	Over $85,651 to $178,650 at 28%
Calculation	8700 * 0.10	(35350 - 8700) * 0.15	(70000 - 35350) * 0.25	N/A
Amount	$ 870.00 +	$ 3,997.50 +	$ 8,662.50 +	
Total Federal Tax	$ 13,530.00			

State (Virginia):

	Up to $3,000 at 2%	Between $3,001 and $5,000 at 3%	Between $5,001 and $17,000 at 5%	Over $17,000 at 5.75%
Calculation	3000 * 0.02	(5000 − 3000) * 0.03	(17000 − 5000) * .05	(70000 − 17000) * 0.0575
Amount	$ 60.00 +	$ 60.00 +	$ 600.00 +	$ 3047.50 =
Total State Tax	$ 3,767.50			

Total Income Tax in Virginia: $ 17,297.50

3) $27,000 salary in Massachusetts

Federal:

	Up to $8,700 at 10%	Between $8,701 and $35,350 at 15%	Between $35,351 and $85,650 at 25%	Over $85,651 to $178,650 at 28%
Calculation	8700 * 0.10	(27000 - 8700) * 0.15	N/A	N/A
Amount	$ 870.00 +	$ 2,745.00 +		
Total Federal Tax	$ 3,615.00			

State (Massachusetts): Flat Tax Rate of 5.3% = 27000 * .053 = **$ 1,431.00**

Total Income Tax in Massachusetts: $5,046.00

Which should you use?

Buying gum and milk at the convenience store.	☑ Cash If you are buying small items then this is the best method. You can pay with a debit card but the fee will inflate the price by about 10-15%.
Taking your best friend out to dinner for his/her birthday.	☑ Credit Card If you have the cash available, then you can pay that way but usually a birthday dinner is more costly and you can take advantage of any rewards program you may have on your card.

Buying groceries for the week.	☑ Debit Card You can pay by cash if you have that much. You can pay by credit card if you don't have enough in your bank account. Debit card is best because any fee for the withdrawal would be small in comparison to the amount of the groceries. (It is a week's worth after all.)
Buying gas.	☑ Credit Card Assuming you are filling the tank, the amount can be around $40-$75 dollars. You can; however, pay with cash or debit if you have it available.
Paying the hydro bill.	☑ EFT Online banking is the way to go (assuming you complete the transaction in time) so that you have an electronic record. You can also pay by check via mail or directly at the bank but it is less convenient.
Making a donation to charity.	☑ Check Ideally, a check gives you a record that you made the donation. This is advantageous so that you can verify whether you receive your tax receipts for donations next Spring. You can also pay by credit card but it will be hard to remember if you received a receipt come tax return season.
Paying your rent.	☑ Check Never pay cash unless you get a receipt. With checks, you can have proof that the landlord received payment when he cashes it. Landlords will rarely take credit cards or any other payment.
Getting your car washed at the annual charity car wash.	☑ Cash Because you won't be getting a tax receipt, cash is the best way for both you and the charity.

Going to McDonald's.	☑ Cash
	While McD's does accept debit and credit cards, the most economical is cash for this small amount of money.
Buying an iPod.	☑ Credit card
	Most credit cards provide automatic insurance on electronics. Plus a $200 iPod will earn you some reward points if your credit card is linked to a reward program.

Average Daily Balance Exercise

Try to figure out what the monthly charge would be based an *annual* interest rate of 28% on the following figures: (see Appendix D for the answer.)

Dates of the month	Balance
1st to 7th inclusive (7 days)	$ 500.00
8th to 14th inclusive (7 days)	$ 750.00
15th to 22nd inclusive (8 days)	$ 900.00
23rd to 31st inclusive (9 days)	$1,400.00

Answer:

First calculate the average daily balance for the month based on the table above.

Calculation:
(7 x 500) + (7 x 750) + (8 x 900) + (9 x 1400) / 31
= (3500 + 5250 + 7200 + 12600) / 31
= 28550 / 31
= 920.97 is the average daily balance

Now calculate the monthly rate:
28% / 12 = 2.33%

Now calculate the monthly charge:

920.97 x .0233 = $21.46

Glossary

401(k)
Type of retirement savings account set up by your employer that allows tax-deferred contributions. Some employers match employee contributions as a benefit of employment.

Annual Percentage Rate (APR)
The yearly rate of interest that banks charge to loan money through cash advances on your credit card, charging items on your credit card, financing a car, getting a mortgage, etc.

ATM
Automated Teller Machine (also known as ABM – Automated Banking Machine) through which you can deposit, withdraw, transfer and pay bills at any time of the day.

Automatic Withdrawal Plan
A regular (monthly, bi-weekly, etc.) transfer set up to automatically withdraw money from one account and deposits it in another account. For example, set up for $200 on the first of every month to be repeatedly withdrawn from your savings account and deposited to your IRA account without your intervention.

Average Daily Balance
Adding each day's balance and then dividing that total by the number of days in the billing cycle.

Balance Transfer
Moving unpaid debt from one credit card to another.

Benefits
Extra incentives provided by your employer including life insurance, health insurance, employer 401(k) contributions, etc. These benefits are usually partially paid by the employer and the other portion is deducted from your paycheck.

Canada Savings Bond
A government investment instrument offered once a year that can be purchased at banks and trust companies.

Cash Advance Fee
A fee charged by your bank for using their credit card to withdraw cash.

Certificates of Deposit
Certificates of Deposit (CD's) are one of the safest investment vehicles out there. If you want to be at the low end of the risk/reward spectrum, CD's might be the right choice.

Checking Account
A bank account that allows you to write checks on. Usually at a lower interest rate than savings accounts.

Compound Interest
When earned interest is added to the principal so that future interest is calculated on both the principal and past interest earned.

Credit Available	Your credit limit minus your outstanding balance on your credit card.
Credit Card	A card that allows the owner to purchase items and services based on the owner's promise to pay in a timely manner. When the entire balance is not paid on time, then a sizable interest fee is charged monthly (usually between 14-29% apr).
Credit Limit	The maximum amount that you are allowed to charge to your credit card.
Credit Report	Also known as "Credit History". A record of an individual's past borrowing and repaying history, including information about late payments and bankruptcy.
Credit Score	A number that indicates a person's level of ability to repay debts.
Daily Rate	Your annual interest rate divided by 365 (number of days in a year).
Debit Card	A card that provides an alternative to cash as the funds are automatically withdrawn from your bank account when used.
Electronic Fund Transfer	Transferring money through online, email or money transfer service operators (e.g. Western Union).
Email Transfer	Transferring money from one person's account to another person's account through email. Accessible from your bank's website. There is usually a fee per transaction to send the money but not to receive it.
FAFSA	Free Application for Federal Student Aid
FCBA	Fair Credit Billing Act is a federal law to protect consumers from unfair billing practices to "open ended" accounts such as credit card accounts.
Federal Income Tax	The amount of money deducted from your salary based on your level of income that goes to the federal government to pay for national projects such as FBI, national defence, NPR, immigration, international relations, Medicare, Social Security, etc.
FDIC	Federal Deposit Insurance Corporation – an independent agency from the federal government that insures bank deposits up to $250,000.

FICA	Federal Insurance Contributions Act is a federal law requiring a deduction from paychecks and income that goes toward the Social Security program and Medicare.
Finance Charge	Fee(s) for using a credit card including interest on unpaid balance and annual fees.
Fixed Annuities	A fixed annuity is a contract with an insurance company. You give them your money to manage, and in exchange they pay you a guaranteed return. Usually the interest on a fixed annuity is tax deferred. Fixed annuities are usually not liquid, which means you will not have easy access to the funds like you do with a bank savings account or money market account.
Government Issues Securities	Investments issued by the U.S. Government are considered very safe. These include things like Series EE/E or I Savings Bond as well as Treasury Bonds, Notes and Bills. You can purchase these safe investments by opening an account directly with the Treasury and investing as little as $25 for savings bonds and as little as $100 for Treasury Bonds, Notes and Bills.
Grace Period	Interest-free time a bank allows between the transaction date and the billing date.
Grant	Financial aid, often based on financial need that does not need to be repaid (unless, for example, you withdraw from school and owe a refund).
Gross Income	Total amount of income that you made before any taxes or deductions are taken out.
Identity Theft	Fraud that involves someone pretending to be someone else in order to steal money or other items. It can involve the stealing of personal information of the victim to create credit cards or get bank loans in the victim's name. The victim is then responsible for paying back any debts incurred even if s/he knew nothing of the scheme.
Interest	A fee paid for the use of money. In the case of a savings account, the bank pays the account holder for the "use" of his/her money. In the case of a loan, the borrower pays the bank interest for the use of the bank's loan.
Investment	Financial instruments that allow you increase (and sometimes decrease) your money.
IRA	Investment Retirement Account - A tax deductible investment account which delays some income tax to a period of

retirement when one's income is expected to be lower and, therefore, at a lower tax rate.

Medicaid
A health program for certain people and families with low incomes and resources managed by state governments but funded by both state and federal governments.

Medicare
A national social insurance program that guarantees access to health insurance for Americans ages 65 and older and younger people with disabilities.

Minimum Monthly Balance
Bank accounts that will waive service fees if you keep a minimum amount of cash in your account at all times.

Minimum Wage
The lowest amount for an hourly wage allowed by law. This wage is different for each state/territory.

Money Market Accounts
Money market funds are a popular cash management tool and although they are not as safe as a bank savings account or certificate of deposit, they are still considered a secure place to park cash.

Mutual Fund
A collection of different financial investments packaged in one fund. As an investor, you would purchase shares in the fund as opposed to the individual stocks that make up the fund.

Net Income
The amount of your salary that you can spend after taxes and deductions are taken out by your employer on behalf of the government.

Online Banking
An internet-based method to conduct financial transactions using your account(s) to pay bills, transfer money, print statements, etc. through a bank's secure website.

Over-the-limit Fee
Fee charged to the credit card owner for exceeding the credit limit.

Pay period
Period of time of employment in which your salary is paid. For example, if you get a paycheck every two weeks, your pay period is bi-weekly.

Payday Loan
A small, short-term loan that a borrower uses to cover expenses until the next payday. The borrower writes a check to the lender for the amount of the loan plus fees and the lender deposits the check on the borrower's next payday. Also known as a cash advance.

Payroll Deductions	Amount withheld from gross salary to pay for taxes and benefits.
Pell Grant	A federal grant for undergraduate students with financial need.
Periodic Rate	An interest rate described in relation to a specific amount of time (e.g. monthly rate).
Pharming	The redirection of internet traffic of a seemingly legitimate website to a bogus website.
Phishing	The fraudulent attempt to obtain personal information by using emails or SMS pretending to be from a legitimate website, payment processors or IT Administrators.
Principal	The original amount of money by which interest is calculated from.
Roth IRA	Type of Investment Retirement Account funded with after-tax earnings. Because of this, earnings grow tax-free and can be withdrawn tax-free as long as the account is open for five years and you're age 59½ or older.
Scholarship	Money awarded to students based on academic or other achievements to help pay for education expenses. Scholarships generally do not have to be repaid.
State Income Tax	The amount of money based on your level of income that is deducted from your salary that goes to your State government to pay for state projects such as health care, infrastructure, education, justice, etc.
Safe Deposit Box	A metal box in a bank rented by you to house valuables (jewellery, stock certificates, etc.) for security reasons. Only you and the bank have a key to access the box.
Savings Account	A bank account that allows you to withdraw and deposit cash and checks. You cannot write checks from this account. It earns a nominal interest rate.
Secured Card	A credit card that is insured with a savings account in case the credit card owner is unable to pay the credit card debt. In this case, the debt will be paid by the savings account.
Simple Interest	The interest earned on the principal investment only.
SMishing	The cell phone text message version of phishing.

Social Security	A federal program of social insurance and benefits developed that include retirement income, disability income, Medicare and Medicaid, and death and survivorship benefits. Social Security is one of the largest government programs in the world, paying out hundreds of billions of dollars per year.
Stocks	Shares in a company.
Stored Value Card	Gift card issued by retailers to be used as an alternative to a non-cash gift. Amount on card is determined by the purchaser of the card at the time of purchase.
Teaser Rate	A below-the-market interest rate offered to entice new credit card customers.
Traditional IRA	An individual retirement account (IRA) that allows individuals to direct pre-tax income, up to specific annual limits, toward investments that can grow tax-deferred (no capital gains or dividend income is taxed). Withdraws begin at age 59 1/2 and are mandatory by 70 1/2.
Variable Interest Rate	An interest rate that fluctuates with other interest rates in the market.
Vishing	The telephone version of phishing.
Work Study	A federal student aid program that provides part-time employment while you are enrolled in school to help pay your education expenses.

www.ingramcontent.com/pod-product-compliance
Lightning Source LLC
Chambersburg PA
CBHW081152270326
41930CB00014B/3119

* 9 7 8 0 9 9 1 6 8 6 1 0 0 *